Dear Colleague

University of Minnesota Press
Minneapolis / London

Dear Colleague

Common and Uncommon Observations

Yi-Fu Tuan

Published by the University of Minnesota Press
111 Third Avenue South, Suite 290
Minneapolis, MN 55401-2520
http://www.upress.umn.edu

Library of Congress Cataloging-in-Publication Data

Tuan, Yi-fu, 1930–
    Dear colleague : common and uncommon observations / Yi-fu Tuan.
        p.   cm.
    ISBN 0-8166-4055-6
    I. Title.
    AC8.T745   2002
    081—dc21   2001005285

Printed in the United States of America on acid-free paper

The University of Minnesota is an equal-opportunity educator and employer.

12 11 10 09 08 07 06 05 04 03 02   10 9 8 7 6 5 4 3 2 1

Contents

Introduction

To be alive is to have hope, and to a writer, no matter how old, hope is belief in one more work yet to be written, another book that is somehow the capstone or distillation of all that has been written before. At the time I was finishing my autobiography (*Who Am I?*), I thought this was it—my capstone or distillation. But even before the page proof came to me, I began to contemplate another work to complement the autobiography with an approach both more impersonal in the sense that it would be directed more at the world, and more personal in the sense that it would be made up of my deeply felt yet somewhat idiosyncratic observations and experiences, the sum of which constitutes a life.

In every life, each waking hour is filled with observations and experiences. Almost all soon disappear. But not all. Why some are retained, or considered worthy of retention, is a mystery—the mystery of self and its world. Over a period of more than thirty years, first in Minneapolis, Minnesota, then in Madison, Wisconsin, I have kept blank-page books in which to record my encounters with objects and persons, ideas and events that impress me at the time as significant. My encounters have taken place in two closely interwoven worlds—that of literature and that outside it, commonly though misleadingly called "real."

In the world of literature, I have read narrowly to become a technically competent geographer—and a geographer is what I am in academic pigeonholing. More important, I have read broadly to be a better and wiser human being. To my mind, the two—wiser human being and better geographer—go together, for I have come to see human geography increasingly as a moral science, the study not only of how people live but also of how they have succeeded or failed to live up to the precepts of their culture. In my broad reading, I almost always have a pencil in hand to underline passages that make me pause. I do this with scholarly books, novels, collections of short stories and poems. Fair enough. But I do the same with articles in newspapers and magazines that are usually considered ephemera. Scholarly works, both those of a philosophical and those of a technical nature, have trained my mind and prepared me to walk with other professionals on the high road of learning. As for the lighter works—and, for me, these include fiction and journalistic reporting—I am somewhat surprised to discover, in retrospect, that they have done at least as much for my intellectual growth. They have tempted me to veer onto unmarked trails. Following them is risky. I have made mistakes and have had to return to the high road, grateful that it is always there to latch onto for security and respectability. But a few of these trails have opened up new horizons. Along with other incautious spirits, I have returned to them again and again so that, in time, what were once mere trails became respectable roads themselves.

Outside of written works, I pause now and then to reflect on major events in the world, in my family, and in my own life. Their conjoined influence has made me into the type of person I am—a Chinese American, an academic, a middle-class professional. It does not, however, explain my differentness, the causes of which lie elsewhere—in my genetic makeup, no doubt, and in the myriad small happenings, individually distinctive or distinctive in combination, that have converged upon me. The result is that I see and respond to the world not quite as others do. A man teaches his dog how to beg. What's noteworthy about that? Yet the image sticks in my mind and insists that I make something of it. The same goes with other minor happenings, such as seeing an overweight woman with varicose veins struggling with her shopping bags, or hearing a child at the Minnesota Zoo asking a middle-aged man (me), "Where is your mommy?"

Of the numerous images from literature and life that I have inexplicably retained, a few could be used for an article or a book: they were the trails that turned into roads, to use my earlier metaphor. The vast majority, however, had no such potential, at least, not for me. So I thought of using them in social conversation. Between sips of Pepsi, I would drop an image (idea or anecdote) in the hope that it would be taken up and developed by people more imaginative than I. Unfortunately, at a research university, real conversations are few and far between. To overcome this frustrating lack of verbal outlet, I worked my images into short letters, which I sent biweekly to friends and colleagues in Minnesota, Wisconsin, and elsewhere. The letters have been well received—so much so that my reputation seems to rest as much on their rumored quality as on actual achievements (such as they are) in my published papers and books.

Over the years, the letters have accumulated to a pile several inches thick. In striking contrast to private correspondence, the reading of which (even letters that bear good news) invariably saddens me with its grave-cloths odor, these more public utterances and commentaries (even those that touch on the intimate or the sad) have a different feel. Many are indeed dated and many are and probably have always been vapid, but a fair number seem to me to have retained their flavor or their contemporary relevance. In my old age, I see them—perhaps overfondly—as passages that I have underlined in a book of life. Will they spark recognition in other people? I wonder, for in reading library books I seldom find passages underlined by a previous reader that are just those I myself would have underlined. But when I do find such passages I feel reassured, confirmed, and happy, as one would at the threshold of a promising friendship.

The anthology format that I have adopted for this book invites the reader to browse. Be my guest! It would please me to know that the book can serve as a genial companion in the airport waiting room, competing successfully with CNN sound bites on ubiquitous television screens. On the other hand, I am offering a life, and a life is more than odd opinions and events sewn together between book covers. For all their diversity and seeming disconnectedness, they should show some sort of pattern, add up to some sort of whole. True, critics in our time have faulted biographies and autobiographies for just that. Life, they say, is full of rough edges, abrupt turns, and contradictions. I agree if this view is not carried too far, for life is not chaos either. So, perhaps the anthology format provides an unexpected solution. As portrait, it bears comparison with a cubist work of art. Unlike the traditional portrait, which shows someone to whom you may offer a cup of tea, the cubist portrait doesn't provide that kind of illusion. Its conflicting points of view don't, superficially, add up or cohere. Yet, arguably, it is a truer simulacrum of a human being.

In the present work, I have grouped observations and thoughts under topical headings to facilitate access. The topics themselves are arranged to follow a path that leads from nature and human nature, through society and culture, geography and history, morality and religion, to stages of life and a sense of ending. This path is not, of course, a life path. Yet it is suggestive of one. In any case, it offers an overall structure and direction, the existence of which will (I hope) tempt some readers to do more than just dip randomly into the book, but rather take the trouble to read it—even with much skipping—from beginning to end. The reward? Well, they will get to know one person and his world better. It doesn't sound like much, yet I think the effort worthwhile—as worthwhile as getting to know stock options, baseball, or a cat. Knowing another person and his world is, of course, more difficult. Even under the most favorable circumstances—two chairs rocking side by side on the porch or a leisurely dinner by the fireplace—we seldom have the courage or patience to probe below surface conventions and pleasantries. Meanwhile, time runs out and we die.

Nature

In my sixteen years as a resident in Madison, I have sat almost daily in the Lakefront Cafe of Memorial Union and watched the changing scene over Lake Mendota. Only yesterday, however, did it occur to me to wonder what I would see if I were in a submersible at the bottom of the lake's cold murky depth, where sunlight never penetrates. And I am a geographer! How extraordinarily limited—and conventional—one's perception is. We are very much creatures of the surface, condemned to superficiality even in imagination and thought.

Strange to think that we may know more about the surface of Venus, thanks to the Magellan Survey of 1990, than about the surface of the earth, so much of which is covered by water. What do we know of underwater topography? How much of it has been seen by human eyes? The experience of human beings striving to pierce the ocean dark in a submersible might be compared to "travelling across Asia by oil-lit hansom cab with the condition of a Dickensian fog outside," as James Hamilton-Paterson wrote in *The Great Deep*. In the absence of knowledge, our imagination works to populate the ocean deep with monsters even more bizarre than those that were once thought to dwell beyond the margins of the inhabited world.

Gravity presses us relentlessly to earth. By evening we are a bit shorter than we were at sunrise. Our own weight punishes us with painful sores when we are confined too long in bed. As I stand nursing a glass of lukewarm ginger ale at an interminable cocktail party, I wish I had extra hands with which to hitch up my loose-fitting garment of skin and flesh.

Still, I say, "If you love nature, you must also love gravity," as Antoine de Saint-Exupéry learned to do. In the 1920s, he piloted his small airplane to deliver mail to remote places in North Africa. One night, after flying many hours, the airplane developed engine trouble and Saint-Exupéry was forced to land it on a bleak plateau in the middle of nowhere. He got out, looked about in a daze, found a smooth spot, and sprawled out on his back, utterly exhausted. A few hours later he woke up, and for a fearful moment thought he was about to fall into a pitch-dark abyss. The next instant he remembered gravity—how firmly and reassuringly it attached his spread-eagle self to Mother Earth.

Vertigo of space is common enough. Stand at the edge of a cliff and one can suddenly feel dizzy, about to fall—about to be drawn into the yawning space. Do people ever experience vertigo of time? Very rarely, I should think, because time, unlike space, is not something that one can see. Its vastness has to be imagined. I have known how it feels to be dizzy in the presence of time only once, when I lived in New Mexico. One day I decided to visit El Moro National Monument, not far to the west of Albuquerque. The monument is noted for the signatures, some dating back to the seventeenth century, that Spanish explorers carved on the flanks of a sandstone mesa. This mesa was once attached to others in the neighborhood to form one large plateau. Streamfloods had cut into the plateau, and the retreat of the valley walls produced a landscape of discrete "tables" or mesas. What caused the walls to retreat? Weathering, rainwash, and wind. As I looked at the signatures, now protected from the elements by glass plates, and then looked at the nearest next mesa—shimmering in the noon glare—about a mile away,

I suddenly felt the vertigo of time. In three hundred years of history, long by human standards, weathering and rainwash had not pushed the cliff back far enough to wipe out the signatures; yet over a period that geologists call Quaternary—a period of no great length from their point of view—the cliff had retreated by perhaps half a mile. While I was ruminating thus at the foot of the mesa, time, normally a manageable gap, suddenly opened up like the Grand Canyon, tempting me to dive in. After this dizzying and slightly sickening experience, I wonder how people can possibly find geological scenery relaxing. Or, rather, I know how they can: by attending to landscape, which, however vast, is always bridgeable and, simultaneously, suppressing all unwelcome knowledge of time. Time is the ultimate wilderness.

When I was a child, my favorite diorama in Sydney's natural history museum was one that showed dinosaurs lounging at the edge of the Cretaceous sea. One dinosaur had a foot raised, as though to step into the water, and its long neck was pointed toward the horizon, as though in appreciation of the setting sun and the brilliantly illuminated sky. Bordering the beach were all kinds of vegetation. I did not doubt as a child, and I have no doubt now, that paleontologists worked hard to get the scene right. But right for whom? Not for the dinosaurs, for these giant reptiles did not have the eyes or brain to see a landscape of beach, sea, and sky. Only human beings could organize reality that way. But there were no human beings in the Cretaceous period! So what am I to conclude? That the diorama is impossible—that it is pure fiction?

Saint Teresa of Avila (1515–82) isn't going to be a very helpful or sympathetic weather forecaster, for, in her opinion, "There is no such thing as bad weather. All weather is good because it is God's." Saint Columba (521–97) didn't recognize bad weather either. Or, rather, he welcomed it without exception. On the desolate island of Iona, he spoke fondly of his "dear cell, in

3

which I have spent such happy hours, with the wind whistling through the loose stones and the sea spray hanging on my hair!"

Hermits of Egypt and Cappadocia in the third and fourth centuries were among the earliest lovers of wilderness: they rejoiced in the austere beauty of the desert, but also in the wild beasts, with whom they established relationships of mutual trust and regard. A hermit removed the thorn from the paw of a wounded lion and then, instead of converting it into a pet, sent it back, with its dignity intact, to the wilderness. (Of course, the details were made up. But the ideal was there.) Only in our time do we find something similar. I think of those marine biologists who dedicate their skill to restoring a stranded and wounded whale to health, and then returning it to its companions in the ocean. Isn't this the sort of dominion over creatures that God intended us to exercise?

Since time immemorial, wise men have said, "Live in the present, for that's all you really have. The past is gone and the future is not yet." Maybe that's good advice, but, as we all know, it is almost impossible to follow. Except, thank God, in the case of weather, which forces us to live in the present. I was reminded of this when I walked State Street in Madison in steamy heat. Why couldn't I cool myself with thoughts of autumn winds that might descend on us next week, if not tomorrow? Why couldn't I chill myself with memories of last winter's snow and ice? It couldn't be done. Yet I know how easy it is for me to shudder *now* with memory of last week's humiliation and in anticipation of next week's difficult task.

Contrary to popular belief, the Old rather than the New Historians are more respectful of nature. Old Historians took for granted that mountains and deserts, blizzards and floods—the nature they knew—were an overwhelming presence and force;

and so to them a single transcontinental railroad, built with so much human ingenuity and sweat, was hardly more than a thin pencil line drawn on erasable bond. By contrast, New Historians see nature as a frail old lady on her last legs and their own species as muscle-bound, swaggering adolescents. Indeed, some New Historians seem to believe that not only sheer physical power— not only "sticks and stones"—but also words can break nature's bones.

A human being can go blind, lose a limb or two, or a third of the brain, and yet in time adjust so well that these losses are barely missed. The same would seem to apply to external nature. Suppose, for reasons of pollution and urban glare, we can no longer see the stars. W. H. Auden, for one, honestly admits that he would learn to look at an empty sky and appreciate its "total dark sublime," though this might take him a while.

By 10,000 B.C., human beings had spread themselves all over the world—except on ice caps and the highest mountaintops. Do we owe this success to brawn or brain? Human beings, as physical anthropologists have pointed out, are large (only sixty animal species are larger), exceptionally strong, and flexible. Moreover, they are endowed with teeth and a digestive system that can take advantage of an extraordinary range of foods. When it comes to physical strength and flexibility, what other animal can measure up to the athletes who participated in the 1999 Triathlon? They swam 2.4 miles, biked 112 miles, and then ran 26.2 miles. Winning time was eight hours, seventeen minutes, and seventeen seconds—three hours less than the winning time in 1978, according to *National Geographic* (September 2000). To account for the success, the brain must be factored in, for it is the brain that endows human beings with purpose, dedication, and the mental power to analyze performance with a view toward improvement.

The Russian Sergei Didik's world record for weight lifting is 575 pounds—a little more than the weight of five average eighteen-year-old American girls. What other animal can match the feat? Can even the strongest elephant lift twice its own weight? Can a donkey carry another donkey on its back?

~•

K'ang-hsi, emperor of China from 1661 to 1722, was an avid hunter. He is quoted by Jonathan D. Spence in *Emperor of China: Self-Portrait of K'ang-hsi:* "Since childhood, with either gun or bow, I have killed in the wild 135 tigers and 20 bear, 25 leopards, 20 lynx, 14 tailed *mi* deer, 96 wolves, and 132 wild boar, as well as hundreds of ordinary stags and deer."

How's this for blood lust? By the end of the twentieth century, hunting in China has become ridiculously tame. At the Country Hunting Park in Danang, close to the Yalu River, tourists can try their hand at killing "wild" quail, pigeons, pheasants, and rabbits, reports Peter Hessler in *The New Yorker* (August 7, 2000). So as not to overtax the hunters' skill, the animals are tethered to the ground. For one yuan, tourists can shoot at them with either a .22-caliber rifle or a bow and arrow. They are allowed to eat anything they kill, thereby experiencing to the full value of the yuan how it feels to be a mighty hunter.

~•

Climbing up the dark and narrow staircase of a Cambridge college, young Bertrand Russell encountered another undergraduate who, on his way down, declaimed in a hypnotic voice,

> Tiger! Tiger! burning bright
> In the forests of the night,
> What immortal hand or eye
> Could frame thy fearful symmetry?

The effect on Russell was overwhelming. For a moment the rationalist in him was quite subdued. Some sixty years later, the American poet James Dickey said in *Sorties* that one of the saddest moments in his life was something he merely read in a newspaper. American troops were bivouacked somewhere in Vietnam. "A tiger came out of the jungle during the night and tried to seize one of the soldiers and he leapt up, grabbed his machine gun, the other soldiers grabbed their weapons—rifles, machine guns, grenades—and all turned on the tiger and blew and shot him almost into nothingness. Why is this so sad? But it is, it is."

The Polish poet Czeslaw Milosz writes to the American poet Thomas Merton: "Every time you speak of Nature, it appears to you as soothing, rich in symbols, as a veil or curtain. You do not pay much attention to torture and suffering in Nature." This is a fairly typical example of a hard-nosed European accusing an American of tipping toward sentimentality whenever nature is invoked. But isn't there much nature sentimentality in Boris Pasternak? Yes. Milosz excuses him, however, because he, unlike Merton, has had to bear "the pressure of historical ruthlessness" (*Striving towards Being: The Letters of Thomas Merton and Czeslaw Milosz*).

Scientific literature is free of the gush so common in popular nature writing. "Some macaques (*Macaca irus*) hold a rival under water for so long that it drowned. Some swimming birds, particularly swans, also adopt these tactics to drown members of small species, gripping them by the bill and holding them under water until they are dead" (Heini Hediger). "Rhesus monkeys kill rhesus monkeys at far higher rates than soldiers were killed in our Civil War" (S. L. Washburn). "The genuine rabbit (as distinct from the Easter Bunny) fights almost nonstop, the males for access to females and the females for good breeding sites. Females dig out the nests of their rivals and kill young rabbits, and they murder juveniles who wander onto their territory. Even the young are not as sweet as one imagines. Nicola Webb of the University of East Anglia describes 'balls of fluff at six weeks old beating hell out of one another'" (*Science*, December 15, 1989).

What about dolphins? Perhaps because of the upward turn of their mouth, which produces a perpetual grin, people have fallen for them since antiquity. The Greeks reported altruism in dolphins, claiming that they had rescued seafarers. Modern Americans believe that they are smarter than dogs and are at least as smart as chimpanzees. New Agers have predictably gone over the top: for them meeting a dolphin is a spiritual experience. Alas, science once again seeks to destroy a fond fantasy. Dolphins, it would appear, can be the cold-blooded killers of their own young. They have been observed to bite, hit, and butt into the air calves for as long as an hour, or until they die. Why is not yet clear. Scientists speculate that the killers might be male dolphins trying to destroy rival offspring and free up females for their own use (*New York Times*, July 6, 1999).

Homosexual rape? Consider the Acanthocephalan worms. "Homosexual rape results in the male victim having the genital region sealed off with cement and effectively removed from the reproductive population. Sperm and cement are transferred to females during copulation, but apparently only cement is transferred to males during homosexual rape." (*Science*, July 1, 1977)

Bestiality? Sounds reprehensible. Yet Ned Rorem, the American composer, tells of a socialite confessing loudly at a party to having spent a whole night in bed copulating with a mosquito.

Even basic attitudes can change fairly rapidly. "Nature is benign; human beings are wicked" is a common attitude, especially among the young, in the last decades of the twentieth century. Yet, earlier, quite the opposite attitude was taken up without irony or self-consciousness. For evidence, I offer Apsley Cherry-Garrard, a member of the Scott expedition to the South Pole who wrote a book called *The Worst Journey in the World* (1922). The "worst journey" was not, as one might expect, the trip to the

Pole but a side trip in the depth of winter to pick up a few emperor penguin eggs. Both trips were made, so Cherry-Garrard believed, in the interest of science. Throughout the book, he recorded superhuman powers of endurance and courage, selflessness, and the will to achieve among his fellow team members. Still more amazing to me is that, throughout the horrible journeys, the men maintained their civility. They eschewed swearing, and I am willing to bet that they never said *fuck*.

By contrast, Cherry-Garrard's comments on the penguin were less than complimentary. Sure, they look adorable, but the "life of an Adélie penguin is one of the most unChristian and successful in the world. . . . Watch them go to bathe. Some fifty or sixty agitated birds are gathered upon the ice-foot, peering over the edge, telling one another how nice it will be, and what a nice dinner they are going to have. But this is all swank: they are really worried by a horrid suspicion that a sea-leopard is waiting to eat the first to dive. The really noble bird, according to our theories, would say, 'I will go first and if I am killed I shall at any rate have died . . . sacrificing my life for my companions'; and in time all the most noble birds would be dead. What they really do is try and persuade a companion of weaker mind to plunge: failing this, they hastily pass a conscription act and push him over."

Sometime in the evolution of the past 3 million years, the semicarnivorous panda switched to an exclusive diet of bamboo. Poorly equipped to digest the new food (they still have the unspecified digestive tract of a carnivore), they must eat a lot of it—twenty-five pounds a day. The bulk of what they eat, since it cannot be used, must be evacuated, which means that in the fourteen waking hours of the day, pandas have to defecate some forty-eight times. Can this be called successful adaptation? Sure, pandas have survived, but what's the good of surviving when time out for fun and games is so constrained by biological necessity?

The total insect population of the world is around a billion billion, making the number of humans (6 billion) seem insignificant. As impressive is their diversity. Over 900,000 insect species have so far been collected, accounting for 56 percent of known life forms. "Without insects every terrestrial ecosystem would collapse and man and almost every other species would rapidly go extinct," says George McGavin, assistant curator of entomology at the University Museum, Oxford. "Insects are the glue that binds the web of life together" (*Oxford Today*, vol. 7, no. 2, 1995). And yet how little we geographers pay attention to them. Environmentalists are not much better. Few have urged respect for mosquitoes or the ants that crawl relentlessly over our picnic basket.

"My mother's voice alone, rising and falling . . . letting itself grow so slack and diffuse it seemed the murmur of nature," writes John Updike. I enjoy the murmur of nature in a park, but also in a coffee shop, where the meaning of words is blurred and I can attend to just their familiar and reassuring sound. Articulate speech is out of place where people seek comfort and intimacy. Whatever poets say, love has never needed verbal eloquence. Baby language is just right in foreplay. As for the sexual act itself, only animal hisses and grunts can do it justice.

At the zoo I realize how much I prefer the solitary animal— the Sheridan tiger and the moose—to the social ones. With solitary animals, I see uniqueness, splendor in the midst of silence. With social animals, I am aware of hierarchy and exclusiveness, the invidious distinction between "us" and "them," and other faults of human society all made painfully obvious by the animals' lack of artifice.

So far as I can see, I am the only unaccompanied visitor to the zoo. Men and women readily go to art galleries and botanical gardens alone, but not to the zoo. While I sit on a bench, sucking an ice-cream cone, watching the school groups and young families go by, a little girl looks at me and asks in a tone that mixes solicitousness with disapproval, "Where is your mommy?"

Nature, to the extent that it means biological life, is a rallying flag for many Americans. But not for all. Gays are a prominent exception. Procreative heat, seething abundance, overpowering greenness have a way of exacerbating their isolation, their sense of being tourists and voyeurs rather than participants. Only in a world of total artifice, all images and glitter, sensation without issue, present without morrow, can they feel at home. Pink is rightly their color, for it is both marginal and somewhat shocking.

I happen to have read two books, both published in 1981, in close succession: Danielo Dolchi's *Sicilian Lives* and Lars Gustafsson's *The Death of a Bee Keeper*. Dolchi tells of a slum dweller who skinned frogs for a living. He felt sorry for the frogs, for they could sense their fate and peed out of fright on his hands. In Sweden, one thousand five hundred miles to the north, Lars Gustafsson writes: "There I stood now listening to the wind, a frog in my hands, as if locked in a cage.... A sour smell came from the swamps on the wooded shore. I clearly felt the frog trembling.... And then suddenly it peed."

Human suffering already gives us the blues. Add to it animal suffering and one feels (or ought to feel) crushed. How comforting it is to know that the universe is overwhelmingly lifeless.

I had the following nightmare. A pile of autumn leaves go on a tour of old people's homes. At every stop they gawk at and express admiration for the spindly legs of the humans, their papery dewlap skins, but, above all, the leaves ooh and ah over the color of people's hair. "Did you see that silver crown over there?" "Look at the lovely copper streaked with gray!" And "This one is still black. Can it be an everblack?" The autumn leaves feel refreshed by what they have seen as they file out of the homes. They chatter merrily and agree that they must return next year. A question they wisely refrain from asking is what the pretty colors signify.

In an ecologically rich environment, one is naturally disposed to see plants and animals as constituting a community. One may also be inclined to think of organic life as made up of generations that project into the future. Individuals die, the group lives on. By contrast, the desert denies both community and continuity. Its message is timelessness—or eternity—rather than long duration, things sustaining and renewing themselves through time. What about life in the desert—for example, flowers that bloom after spring showers? Yes, but they quickly disappear, as though to dramatize the ephemerality of life. In the desert, ruins last longer than they do in humid regions. In this sense, they endure. But they endure as ruins. The desert, so rich in mementos of discontinuity, is consoling to people who, like me, are good for just one season.

Many wild animals have become extinct. Those that remain are not accessible if one lives in a great city. If it is just the thrill of wildness one wants, however, won't a natural history museum do? Forty-seven preteen Girl Scouts were thrilled when they had permission to sleep overnight in the American Museum of Natural History in Manhattan. Some favored a night alone with the dinosaurs. Some chose to sleep in the northeast corner of the Hall of Ocean Life, near the giant squid with those really long slimy arms. A ninety-four-foot blue whale hung from the ceiling. "Of course, my lifelong dream has been to sleep under that whale," a Scout in pink sweatpants opined as she spread out her bedroll. "But, you know, things *can* happen in the wilderness" (*New Yorker*, April 11, 1988).

Sit Jessica. Look how the floor of heaven
Is thick inlaid with the patines of gold;
There's not the smallest orb which thou behold'st
But in his motion like an angel sings,
Still quiring to the young-ey'd cherubims:
Such harmony is in immortal souls;
But, whilst this muddy vesture of decay
Doth grossly close it in, we cannot hear it.
—*The Merchant of Venice*, Act 5, Scene 1

I can imagine young Lorenzo sitting next to Jessica on an evening flight from New York to San Francisco. They have just had dinner and are holding hands when Lorenzo glances out of the window, notices the glittering webs of light over the Midwest, and says, "Look how the floor of the earth is thick inlaid with patines of gold!"

Young people in our time are far more likely to look *down* than up. The immense panoply of heaven, adorned with countless stars, has dropped out of their conception of nature. For them, nature is the earth's biosphere, especially the vulnerable parts that have caught their attention. When they talk about harmonious relationship with nature, they have in mind people adapting to the earth's ecological system, as all other living things do. But in Shakespeare's time, adaptation was far more grandly conceived. To young Lorenzo and Jessica, the harmony to be sought was between the celestial orbs above and the immortal souls below.

Shakespeare did not see nature through a romantic haze. He did not flatter nature; nor did he find nature flattering. In fact, it was precisely nature's straight dealing that he admired:

Are not these woods
More free from peril than the envious court?
Here feel we but the penalty of Adam,
The season's difference; as the icy fang
And churlish chiding of the winter's wind,

Which, when it bites and blows upon my body,
Even till I shrink with cold, I smile and say
"This is no flattery; these are counsellors
That feelingly persuade me what I am."
　　　　　　　　—*As You Like It*, Act 2, Scene 1

I can stand before a giant boulder lost in awe and admiration. What I like about it is its air of immutability. But that does not seem the reason why most young people I know appreciate nature; significantly, by nature they have in mind weather, the seasons, water, plants, and animals—things that change, things whose beauty is typically frail or transient. We human beings know change and frailty as we do not know permanence. We bond naturally with the daffodil, because as Robert Herrick (1591–1674) put it:

We have short time to stay as you,
We have as short a spring;
As quick a growth to meet decay
As you, or anything.

Strolling through the wood, admiring nature, would be anathema—far too genteel—to D. H. Lawrence. Passionate, erotic, even violent response was more to his taste. In *Women in Love*, he had Rupert Birkin take off his clothes to copulate with vegetation. At first, Birkin sat naked among the primroses, "letting them touch his belly, his breasts. . . . But they were too soft. He went through the long grass to a clump of young fir-trees, that were no higher than a man. The soft sharp boughs beat upon him, threw little cold showers of drops on his belly, and beat his loins with their clusters of soft sharp needle. . . . To lie down and roll in the sticky, cool young hyacinths, to lie on one's belly and cover one's back with handfuls of fine wet grass, soft as a breath, soft and more delicious and more beautiful than the touch of any woman; and then to sting one's thigh against the living dark bristles of

14

the fir-bough; and then to feel the light whip of the hazel on one's shoulders, stinging, and then to clasp the silvery birch-trunk against one's breast, its smoothness, its hardness, its vital knots and ridges—this was good, this was all very good, very satisfying."

National parks are supposed to provide solitude. But what is solitude? Well, to Americans, this is not a philosophical question; rather, it is one that polls can address. "A poll shows that tourists tolerate some 30 other people while communing with nature at Delicate Arch [in Utah's Arches National Park]—so its parking lot will be sized accordingly" (*National Geographic,* October 1994). What will Thoreau think?

I tell my geography class about Hutcheson Forest, a sixty-five-acre virgin forest in New Jersey. No one has touched but many have observed it. Richard Forman, a forestry professor, says that it is "probably the single most studied primeval wood on the continent." Students have gone in and emerged with more than a hundred advanced degrees, including thirty-six Ph.D.'s (*New Yorker,* July 6, 1987). After all that intrusive gaze, Hutcheson Forest, even if it remains physically intact, is hardly virgin.

Is there a part of nature that the human mind has not successfully penetrated—and may never successfully penetrate—because it is not equipped to do so? The philosopher Colin McGinn's answer is yes, and it is "consciousness." In his 1999 book *The Mysterious Flame,* he begins with a quotation from a science fiction story in which extraterrestrial scientists captured human beings who, earlier on, had made their presence known by transmitting signals. The scientists discovered, to their astonishment, that human beings, including their brain, are entirely made of meat. Their question (and ours) is, How can meat produce sentience or consciousness, much less the sort of intelligence that can send signals to outer space?

McGinn emphasizes that consciousness is a fact of nature—and the existence of this fact is even less subject to radical doubt than is the existence of, say, a tree or the solar system. Moreover, consciousness is a fairly primitive and common fact of nature, for as soon as organisms developed some sort of brain and a sensory apparatus (eyes, ears, and so on), they were able to experience reality—to have consciousness of it—in a certain way. The scientific question is, How can neurons and neuronal paths (meat!) produce consciousness? We don't have an answer, and this is not because the phenomenon is too complex; in the progressive march of science, we have never been stumped conceptually by mere complexity. So what is the problem? The problem, says McGinn, is that our brain is just not equipped to understand consciousness. The brain did not evolve for that purpose. Rather, it evolved to cope with two principal challenges—social relations and spatial reality. Success in the one led to the establishment of intricate organizations and institutions, and success in the other led to the scientific understanding of everything from neutrinos to galaxies, from the chemical composition of rocks to the physiology and circuitry of the brain.

Should the inability of our brain to understand *all* aspects of nature make us sad? Yes, if our self-esteem depends on omniscience. No, if we yearn for true wilderness—that is to say, a part of nature that is forever beyond our reach—even intellectually.

Until the rise of modern science, nature's utter indifference to human well-being was far too desolating a notion to be entertained anywhere. If experience occasionally gave rise to it, it was quickly squelched. Nature had to be responsive, as human beings were responsive. Even malevolence in nature was preferred, for malevolence could be fought with verbal appeals and propitiatory rites. Even today, football fans, rather than dismiss the downpour that washes out the match as a meteorological fluke, react in frustration and resentment as though it were a deliberate spoiler. Nature cares—perversely! The flood not only destroys, it seeks to destroy. The 1996 movie *Twister* treats the tornado as both villain that chases and big game that is chased. Even the National Weather Service gives human names to tropical storms, in deference to the public's incurable anthropomorphizing need. The natural world will never lose its human face and passion— its poetry—so long as our own nature is not drastically (genetically) altered. Indeed, the move, even in the most advanced societies, seems to be in the other direction—toward tree hugging, animal rights (animal obligations?), and the feeling that rocks and the planet Earth itself are endowed with sentience and will.

"Any small earthquake has some probability of cascading into a large event. [Whether it happens] depends on a myriad of fine details of physical conditions throughout a large volume, and not just in the immediate vicinity of the fault," said an expert at a 1996 London conference (*Science*, March 14, 1997). Knowing all these details with great accuracy is highly improbable. Hence, we may never be able to tell when the next big quake will occur.

I am surprised that a physical system made up of inanimate elements is so resistant to prediction. It makes me think that predicting large events in biological—and, all the more, human— systems is hopeless. No one could have foretold the collapse of the Soviet Union in 1989, for this major quake depended on (to paraphrase the earth scientist) a myriad of fine details of sociopolitical conditions throughout the Soviet empire, and not just in the immediate vicinity of the Kremlin. Even Gorbachev, a man of modest ability—a minor tremor on the political scene— could trigger a quake of the first magnitude.

Here is an alternative genesis myth. When God created human beings and made the earth their abode, he was forced to tag on the universe—quarks and black holes, galaxies and nebulae— because otherwise his large-brained creatures would suffocate intellectually for lack of room to move and explore. God took on more than he had originally planned. He resents the extra work, and that's why he gives his human creatures such a hard time.

Of the numerous stories of how human beings have despoiled nature, it is curious that the following is not more often told. I am reminded of it one day as I sit by a window of Lakefront Cafe, watching an airplane flying across the blue sky. I think to myself, What an extraordinary amount of intelligence is concentrated in that tiny, barely moving dot: passengers reading blockbuster novels, tapping on their laptops, working on crossword puzzles, chatting, and, in the cockpit, pilots examining the bank of dials, consulting charts and schedules, speaking with air controllers miles away. To these acts of intelligence must be added the even more arduous and sustained thinking that has gone into the design and construction of that airplane. In sharp contrast, the immense space that surrounds it is silent and mindless.

At first, I feel an upwelling of pride in human achievement. Then a horrible thought intrudes. I see the airplane as a demon—one of a long line of technological demons—sucking into itself all the mind that was in the universe so that, eventually, it is there and nowhere else. For a long time, from antiquity to the early modern period, people took for granted that the universe, far from being lifeless and silent, was filled with intelligent spirits, of which the sparkling stars were an outstanding example. On earth, too, spirits were everywhere. Human beings were animate and sentient, but so were plants and animals and even certain rocks and bodies of water; human beings were intelligent, but no more so than the ghosts and spirits that were our ancestors' constant companions. And now, what utter desolation confronts me, on earth and in the sky, as I look out of the café's window.

But I exaggerate. The twister in *Twister* still has intelligence—malevolent intelligence!

What is nature made of—fundamentally? Democritus (ca. 460–370 B.C.) offered the hard, materialistic answer: tiny par-

ticles (atoms). He thus distinguished himself from the more abstract and vague answers of his predecessors—Anaxagoras's
"mind" and Empedocles' "harmony and discord." Modern physics
seems to be returning to the earlier positions, at least in degree
of abstractness. For most of the twentieth century, physicists
have been telling us that nature is made up of bundles of energy
rather than particles. Now, it would seem, they go a step further
and say that it is made up of "space"! The latest grand theory in
physics, one that promises to unify quantum physics with Einstein's relativity, is called string theory—and strings are made of
space. What is so appealing about this answer is that it explains
the age-old conundrum of how everything could have come from
nothing. Well, in a sense, everything is nothing. No wonder we
feel unreal at times.

Can miracles happen? Yes, if by miracle one means an interruption—a momentary breaking down—of the natural laws that
govern our universe. Suppose there is more than one universe, as
quite respectable physicists now postulate. A miracle then is the
leaking of an alien universe into our own and therefore unac-
countable (miraculous) according to our own laws. Here is how
I understand the story in greater detail. Until recently, physicists
held that information is never lost. For example, a message is
written in the snow and the snow melts. No problem: the message still exists somewhere in the pattern of water molecules, and
all that needs to be done to restore the message is to reintegrate
backward. Even when information is sucked into a black hole, it
is still not lost, but is held there in a sort of cosmic lockbox. Now,
from 1976 onward, under the influence of Stephen Hawking,
physicists are beginning to believe that black holes are not lock-
boxes, but leaky windows. Information could exit to another universe. And, of course, it could also enter. "A television set could
come out," says physicist Donald Page. Now, *that* would be a miracle by any standard. (See Faye Flan, "Plugging a Cosmic Information Leak," *Science*, March 26, 1993.)

We Americans are a practical people. If we pour money into science, it is because it will yield useful technology and products that can improve or save human lives. High-energy physics may seem, at first, an exception. It isn't, for it can at least be argued that the results of high-energy physics will eventually feed into useful technology. That leaves us with astronomy. Billions have been poured into astronomy in the past fifty years: money keeps coming to it even in straitened times (such as the early 1990s) when the more practical sciences are shortchanged. But why? No one has ever argued for astronomy's usefulness. No one has to. Astronomy tells us about the heavens. Wanting to know about the heavens—their grandeur and sublimity—somehow elevates the human spirit, making us feel even in bad times that we are more than just hapless creatures crawling on, and polluting, the surface of the earth. Moreover, aren't the heavens the last—the true—wilderness, which we can contemplate and admire, but never visit and spoil?

Life, so far as we can tell, is extremely rare in our universe. Strange that so much of it is concentrated on a minor planet of a minor star of a minor galaxy. And of the approximately 50 billion species that have lived on Earth, only one acquired sufficient intelligence to generate civilizations (so says Ernst Mayr). Shouldn't we, in the name of explanatory economy, consider our species way out of line with the known laws of the universe—in short, a miracle?

Civilization and City

Converting nature into city is the most tangible hallmark of civilization. Geographers, perhaps more than planners and other social scientists, tend to see the change almost exclusively in terms of spatial organization and refinement. But we should not forget time. Civilization is—has to be—sensitive to time, for its characteristic activities and works are often of a scale and complexity, involving many people, that require exquisite temporal-spatial coordination. In response to both its own rules and necessity, civilization is under pressure to complete projects within set time periods. In the old days, for example, cosmological ritual might demand that all work cease by winter solstice. In the practical sphere, overflow ditches must be in place and operative before the next predicted flood. At a personal level, the potentate, conscious of his own mortality, may insist that his monumental tomb be finished within two years. Time is recognized as a scarce resource that must not be wasted.

Individuals in civilized societies can be almost neurotic about not wasting time. Here are three recorded cases: one from antiquity, one from the early modern period, and the last from our day.

Pliny the Elder was a Roman naturalist who died while observing the eruption of Vitruvius in 79 A.D. His nephew wrote: "I remember once his reader (at a banquet) having mispronounced a word, one of my uncle's friends at the table made him go back to where the word was and repeat it again; upon which my uncle said to his friend, 'Surely you understood it?' Upon acknowledging that he did, 'Why then,' said he, 'did you make him go back again? We have lost more than ten lines by this interruption'" (*The Letters of Caius Plinius Caecilius Secundus*).

John Dee (1527–1608) was a distinguished geographer and mathematician. Describing his years as a student at St. John's College, Cambridge, Dee wrote: "I was so vehemently bent to study, that for those years I did inviolably keep this order; only to sleep four hours every night; to allow to meat and drink (and some refreshing after) two hours every day; and of the other eighteen hours all (except the time going to and being at divine service) was spent in my studies and learning" (Francis Yates, *Theatre of the World*).

Frederick Mosteller, a former president of the American Association for the Advancement of Science, is a prolific and highly esteemed statistician. One way Mosteller manages to be so productive is to severely regiment time. A sign at his office asks, "What have I done for statistics in the past hour?" And he tells a colleague that he once kept a record of what he did every fifteen minutes of the day (*Science*, April 27, 1979).

We say that Louis Le Vau and Louis XIV built Versailles. But, of course, an army of workers of different skills—architects and painters, gardeners and hydraulic engineers, furniture makers and seamstresses (the list can go on and on)—contributed to its construction. We say that George Lucas made *Star Wars*, but, of course, again an army of workers of different skills—actors and architects, engineers and digital-imaging scientists, stunt men and dressmakers (the list can go on and on)—contributed to its making. Few critics have noted this similarity between monumental architecture and epic movie in using the widest range of materials and skills to create, or re-create, a world.

Civilization builds monuments to last. Many of them, including Versailles, do last. Absent the social fabric in which they were once embedded, buildings become public sculptures and, as such, they continue to command attention. Making a movie epic requires at least as many skills and meticulous coordination of them as did the making of architectural monuments in earlier times. There is, however, this important difference: even the greatest and most expensive movie epics stand in the public's eye for only a few months and then disappear; if they reappear, they do so as videos and DVDs in private homes. Doesn't this show an extraordinary change in the value that people place on permanence or duration? Modern people do not seem to mind putting huge effort into projects that are essentially of the passing moment. Their nonchalance suggests that they take their power and creativity to be unlimited.

Civilization means excess. With ten fingers, we can count up to ten—good enough to raise us beyond mere survival to comfortable living. So why go further? Why would anyone want to

know the prime numbers the product of which gives $2^{193} - 1$?
Yet some people do. That's the wonder of high civilization.
At Sandia National Laboratories, computation experts took
only 38.3 minutes to come up with the following answer:
13821503 $\times$ 6165444023324834061 6559 $\times$
14732265321145317331 35328283. Now are we all happy? I, for
one, am—possibly out of species pride. We *are* smarter than
chimpanzees, no matter what Jane Goodall says.

Material excess, however, is something else. At a fancy restaurant in Minneapolis, even before I sat down with my fellow
lunchers, I noticed and was offended rather than pleased by all
the work that had gone into just three pats of butter—yellow,
pink, and chocolate—carved into the shape of flowers. At the
buffet table, hillocks of meat and seafood, parterres of vegetables,
and columns of bottled water and wine assaulted my appetite and
killed it. I withdrew to our table and ordered a chicken salad,
trusting in its modest, all-American pedigree. What I got was
another extravagant work of art—a bouquet of crisp lettuce,
asparagus, avocado, and red cabbage, topped by thin slices of
tenderly browned chicken. Even the high quality of the service
managed to give me offense. In the brief moment that my lunch
companions left for a second helping, two waiters came to remove the used plates, substitute clean ones, refill our glasses
with spring water topped by a thin wedge of artfully twisted
lemon, and refold the salmon-colored napkins into blushing
blossoms. I vowed never to return.

Luxury has more to do with sex than with the superfluity and
quality of material possessions. Its old meaning, as Lionel Trilling
reminds us in *Beyond Culture,* is erotic and nothing but erotic: "For
Chaucer and Shakespeare *luxury* meant lust and its indulgence.
Women present themselves to Keats's imagination as luxuries:
'All that soft luxury / that nestled in his arms.' A poem is described as 'a posy / of luxuries, bright, milky, soft and rosy.'" In

patriarchal societies, only men are in a position to enjoy luxuries. Women may lounge in them, but women themselves are part of the "pillowy silkiness" (Keats) that men relish.

The aristocrat, says Jean-Paul Sartre in *Saint Genet*, "eats Nature, and the product he consumes should smell a little of entrails or urine." To a man of taste, the authentic luxury good should have, beneath its glitzy, arty appearance, "the carnal, clinging, humble, organic milky taste of the creature." Machine-made lace can never be a satisfactory substitute for the real article because it cannot replace the lacemaker's "long patience, the humble taste, the eyes that are ruined by the work." Even today, when there is great respect for the kind of perfection that only high technology can achieve, the true luxury good must still carry a hint of organic origins. Manufacturers of Waterford crystal, for example, advertise their product as "Blown by mouth and cut wholly by hand. With heart." Volvo car manufacturers, perhaps imitating Rolls-Royce, stress human labor in their advertisements: "Each body panel is carefully fitted by hand; each seam is hand-burnished. . . . [And] the wood paneling is hand-polished to an elegant gloss." "Hand-burnished" and "hand-polished" suggest that it is the oil and sweat exuding from the human body rather than wax or some chemical product that give the panel its luxurious sheen.

Civilized sensibility and the art of camouflage go together. In western Europe during the seventeenth century and early eighteenth century, improvement in manners was accompanied by an increasing disgust with physical cruelty and the sight of blood. Hence the decks of men-of-war were painted crimson, and red coats spread to the armies to make the effects of bloody battle less visible and fearsome (J. U. Nef, *War and Human Progress*).

Toilets "rise up from the floor like white water lilies," writes Milan Kundera. "Even though the sewer pipelines reach far into our houses with their tentacles, they are carefully hidden from view, and we are happily ignorant of the invisible Venice of shit underlying our bathrooms, bedrooms, dance halls, and parliaments." Civilization is a constant effort to cover up the fact that we shit, often smell bad, sooner or later decay and die. In a well-run modern city—even in its hospitals and funeral homes—all reminders of such unpleasantness (including the poor) are carefully hidden from view.

We denounce technology for standardizing the world. To restore the earlier diversity, what about—for a start—destroying all our eyeglasses? That way each of us can return to his or her unique vision.

Technology has given us the camera. Could Wordsworth have used one? I believe so. Consider the following passage in a letter Wordsworth wrote in 1790: "Ten thousand times in the course of this tour [of the Alps] have I regretted the inability of my memory to retain a more strong impression of the beautiful forms before me, and again and again in quitting a fortunate station have I returned to it with the most eager avidity, with the hope of bearing away a more lively picture" (quoted in Stephen Gill, *William Wordsworth: A Life*).

Parents like to tell stories about their children. Only since the mid-nineteenth century, however, have they been able to do so around snapshots in the family album. There again, how easily we forget our debt to technology and its products! Without the prompting of snapshots, not only do beautiful scenes disappear (as with Wordsworth), but so do the faces of our loved ones.

I am in a Douglas-10, some 30,000 miles above the earth. I try to be grateful for the vapid airline magazine and tasteless chicken, for they are, after all, there for my entertainment and sustenance: people have worked hard on them; they are my world. In sharp contrast, the blue sky of grandeur and beauty, separated from me by a mere glass plate, is instant death. We can contemplate, but cannot live in, perfection.

One extremely cold day (minus forty degrees Fahrenheit), the heating system in my apartment building (the River Towers Condominium in Minneapolis) broke down. The temperature fell steadily as the hours went by. I put on extra clothes. That proved insufficient. My last line of defense was to plug in my electric blanket, wrap it around me, and wait for warmth to seep into my body. I regarded the wire that snaked across the floor as my lifeline. Without it, I fancied I would die like one of those brain-damaged patients kept minimally functioning by modern technology. Then I thought, even under normal conditions, I survived because I was plugged into the outlets of civilization.

Does anyone miss the enclosed phone booth as I do? Its disappearance from American cities in the 1970s is, to me, a sad loss for civilization. Illuminated at night on a dark roadside or a busy street corner, the booth is a reminder that alone and in a strange place, anyone with small change can find the consolation of a friendly voice. A vandalized booth is thus violence against human mutuality, as it is also violence against our animal need for shelter—for a pool of light, warmth, and calm in the midst of natural and human turmoil.

Yet how selfish of me to speak thus. Apparently one reason why the open stand replaced the booth is to make the phone available to the handicapped. So civilization, judged by its degree of consideration for the handicapped, does march forward. Civilization is also technology. Recently, technological ingenuity has created the cellular phone, which can be used in the car or at a coffee-shop table—a big improvement in convenience for those who can afford one. But who is left behind? In the absence of public phones, what will people do who have only coins in their pocket? And what about the social cost—the cost in civility? What about the rudeness of ignoring all your fellow diners—ignoring, too, the dining room's own hard-won architectural ambience—in order to clinch a deal with some disembodied voice on the other side of the ocean?

E-mail is wonderfully efficient, but it is not erotic. Think of a personal letter sent in the old-fashioned way. You seek the sort of paper that reflects the degree of esteem or intimacy. You take time to write. You fold the letter lovingly and put it in an envelope. You apply your own body fluid to the envelope's flap and then to the stamp. It is all too clear that as civilization progresses, human contact shies away from the body: first to go was the hug-and-kiss, then the handshake, and now, with e-mail, the sexy lick.

A mark of high civilization is the institutionalized care of the stranger. In China, it was Buddhism, with its otherworldly values, rather than Confucianism, with its commitment to family and community, that established charitable institutions accessible to all. In the West, the inns and hospitals that catered to the needs of the poor and of travelers during the eleventh and twelfth centuries were inspired in their founding and endowment by the preaching and example of hermits, who were themselves rootless and poor. Later in the thirteenth century, inspiration came from the friars, outstandingly Francis of Assisi. They, too, were footloose: universal charity seemed to go with geographical restlessness.

Looking after our own kind is primal, perhaps instinctive. Looking after the stranger is an ideal and an achievement of people who have routine business dealings away from home and who therefore know what it is like to be out of place and un-protected. In the ancient Greek city, local customs and laws provided protection and means of redress. Beyond the city, they had no force, and the traveler was at the mercy of something far more diffuse—moral feelings. Such feelings could not be trusted to sustain themselves. They required nurturing, which the idea of a transcendental god supplied. To the Greeks, that god was Zeus. When people traveled beyond city gates, they came under the aegis of Zeus. They were "stranger-guests," deserving of cour-teous treatment, as the *Odyssey* repeatedly asserted.

Do you have a favorite period in history, one that you would want to live in if you had the choice? George Orwell (1903–50), a socialist well known for his ardent anti-imperialism, chose, sur-prisingly, late Victorian and Edwardian England, the greatest imperial power of its time. What he liked about England then, for all its political and military hubris, social snobbery, and envi-ronmental horrors, was the retention of a certain amount of "decency and comeliness" (Orwell's favorite words), a lingering belief in the nonarbitrary nature of good and evil, and an ability to say no to strongly tempting but unsavory deeds because they are "not done."

Are decency and comeliness possible in the absence of tran-scendental principle or faith that the Victorians and Edwardians still more or less upheld? Orwell was doubtful. Modern men and women seemed to him brittle and shrill. Even with material affluence, they showed deep insecurity and mistrust—a mistrust that they sought to overcome by legal and contractual means (George Woodstock, *The Crystal Spirit*).

A hundred years later, at the turn of the millennium, post-modern men and women have moved much further in the direction Orwell foresaw and disliked. Faith—religious faith— remains strong, but it is become more social than sacral, more propriety than numinous awe. Good and evil, as shades of gray or matters of taste, have been shorn of their element of strenu-

ousness (William James). As for "decency and comeliness," how
quaint they now sound. Under flexible capitalism, loyalty to institutions is decidedly passé. Trust is a business necessity, time-
bound and contracted for reasons of efficiency.

Yet all is not regress. In some areas, we have actually raised
the bar for civilized behavior. As the twentieth century winds
down, no respectable person would use ethnic slurs or shun the
disadvantaged, keep them not only out of work but also out of
sight. The life of a soldier has suddenly become invaluable. During the First World War, a general thought nothing of sending
thousands to almost certain death. In the Kosovo war of 1999,
the possible loss of even one soldier gives the chairman of the
joint chiefs the willies. True, enemy soldiers are still dispensable.
But civilians on the other side cannot be killed; killing them acci-
dentally would call for repeated expressions of regret.

What kind of a world should we aim at in the twenty-first
century? Not, I suggest, a return to the middle Paleolithic age, as
some extreme social egalitarians and environmentalists desire.
For a more equable distribution of wealth, a return merely to the
year 1800 would do the trick. In that year, the per capita income
in the whole Third World averaged about $200; in China it was
$228; in Western Europe it was $213 (according to Keith
Thomas, *New York Review of Books*, November 22, 1984). And in
that year there were still tropical forests galore.

European visitors to the United States find much to admire
and criticize. One criticism is directed at the phrase "Have a
good day." Visitors are offended by what is, to them, an obvious
insincerity. Yet the same visitors would consider the insincere
courtesies of their own world—"faithfully yours," tipping the
hat to ladies, giving up one's seat to the elderly—as the finest
flowers of civilization; and they would judge attacks upon them
as boorish, a failure to understand that genial words and gestures,
besides elevating the social atmosphere, have practical conse-

quence. What practical consequence? Well, to put it crudely, expressions of goodwill can be cashed. A waiter who has just said to me "Have a good day" makes himself vulnerable to my request for street direction.

In a truly civilized society, when my car breaks down, I can count on the car behind me to stop. Someone will step up to offer help. It is inevitable—just one of those annoying, insincere things that drivers in a truly civilized society do!

I had lunch at a Chinese fast-food restaurant on University Avenue in Madison. When a young couple with a baby finished eating, the man put the paper dishes and plastic forks into the trash bin and the trays on top, as people do at fast-food restaurants. The woman strapped her child into the stroller. The man opened the door for them. And then, to my surprise, he returned to the table and adjusted the chairs to their original positions.

What's going on here? Nothing special. Just your run-of-the-mill good manners in public places. But, if so, what a compliment to American society! Where else does one find it? Paris? London? Beijing? McDonald's exports hamburgers, which can be an offense to European taste. But the deeper offense is that it has had the presumption to export manners.

New York City, having neglected its upkeep in the 1960s and 1970s, was confronted by the task (according to a report of the Joint Economic Committee) of soon having to replace or repair 1,000 bridges, 6,200 miles of streets, 6,000 miles of sewers, 6,000 miles of water lines, 6,700 subway cars, 4,500 buses, 25,000 acres of parks, and hundreds of police and fire stations. Of course, the average citizen understands this: he knows that his own house requires periodic fixing and retouching; he can see that streets are always being barricaded for repairs, that workers are always fixing buildings and bridges. But somehow he cannot shake the curious illusion that all this busyness is temporary and that one day the city will finally be finished, as a sculptural work of art is finished, so that thereafter he and his fellow citizens can just sit back, relax, and enjoy. No such luck, however: a city must always be noisy with pneumatic drilling, must always irritate with its closed streets and detours.

And isn't this a fundamental reason, little acknowledged, why urbanites have historically dreamed of returning to nature—to an environment that doesn't require repair work, that quietly maintains itself? And isn't it ironic that we have come to realize that wild nature, too, requires repair work on our part—periodic burning of the underbrush, periodic reintroduction of fauna that have become scarce, and so on—to maintain its "primeval" character?

New York, New York. Rather than pay an exorbitant price for a Continental breakfast in my hotel, I went to Eat-and-Run on Broadway and Sixty-first Street. The place hummed. Just about every stool at the counter was occupied. Customers and wait-resses kidded one another. I waited to be served. No one, how-ever, took any notice until a young fellow next to me shouted at a passing waitress, "Hey! You are neglecting my buddy!" My order was quickly taken. Thereafter my neighbor ignored me. That, to me, was impersonal, big-city hospitality at its finest.

In my naïveté, I assumed that "the magic of the city" is avail-able to everyone fortunate enough to live in a great metropolis rather than being an experience, with roots in childhood, that is the prerogative only of a certain social class. The child I have in mind is someone who is supposed to be in bed, but who creeps down the stairs in his pajamas and sits on a step in the dark, his eyes focused on a strip of light under the dining room, his ears attentive to chatter and laughter in a world as yet forbidden to him. No working-class child could have had this kind of experi-ence—previsions of excitement in the theater on opening

nights, of poise and ease in chandeliered drawing rooms faintly
imbued with the fragrance of Cuban cigars.

Urbane city life depends on the availability of leisure. During
classical antiquity, the marketplace was the haunt of leisured
Greek men. They gossiped while they shopped, pausing now and
then to discuss politics and philosophy. In the nineteenth century, the arcades of Paris were the haunt of strolling dandies or
flâneurs (Walter Benjamin's word). They too shopped and gossiped. However, when their voices rose in excitement it was not
over the nature of Good and other metaphysical quandaries, but
rather over literature and literary reputations. In present-day
United States, membership in the leisured class has swelled as
never before, and is mostly made up of well-to-do retired people—the *flâneurs* of shopping malls. They are there primarily for
the exercise. When they sit beneath the plastic trees, they are
either silent or they exchange news of aches and pains, the
iniquities of HMOs and nursing homes. Such is progress. What
can one expect when medical science has forced people to live
way beyond threescore and ten?

A test of a civilization is whether one would want to snooze
in its urban parks. Of course, one can snooze anywhere—in the
countryside, in the mountains. But certain elements are lacking
there. For really good snoozing, says *The New Yorker* (November
13, 1989), "you need a city that has enough bustle and clatter
and tension to make a person yearn for a calm green spot." You
need, of course, a park where the dog ordinance is strictly en-
forced, but you also need "a civilized person capable of dropping
his guard and his pretenses and flopping down on the ground
and falling asleep with his mouth open."

Manhattan measures up to many tests of civilization, but it
fails the snooze test. European cities do much better. Rome has
the Villa Borghese; London, Queen Mary's Garden in Regent's
Park; and Copenhagen, Orsteds Parken, arguably the best of all.

Politics and Ideology

With civilization come politics and ideology—explicitly formulated activities and ideas that can be quite controversial. My own are no exception. Strange to think that I can write about sex and religion (as I shall later) without raising the reader's hackles, but not about politics. So, diplomatically, let me start with a noncontroversial, but still interesting (I like to think), commentary.

One of the greatest state-and-religious rituals in history took place on June 2, 1953. I refer to the coronation of Elizabeth II. Among the theatrical gestures that the organizers threw into the works were the donning, Roman style, of the tunic of the emperors; the rendering of homage, feudal style, to the sovereign; the anointing of the queen, modeled after the anointing of King Solomon, with its implied claim to divine authority; and the use of the sacred oil that the Virgin Mary reportedly entrusted to Saint Thomas Aquinas. Henry Fairlie, a hard-nosed political commentator for *The New Republic,* thought he had witnessed, along with 300 million others, something that "one should never see—the terrible prescriptions by which a society holds itself together." Sociologist Edward Shils described the queen, at the moment of anointing, as "a frail creature who has to be brought into contact with the divine and thus transformed into a Queen." The occasion itself was deemed "a great act of national communion" (*Sociological Review,* December 1953).

Democracies are rightly suspicious of public rituals, especially after the travesty made of them by Nazi Germany. Nevertheless, students of society should welcome them as open-stack books to be read and interpreted. How do political regimes differ in practice, aspiration, and ideal? One way to find out is to observe the stage props and activities in celebrations of the collective self. What, for example, is the ratio of balloons to flags, family picnics to triumphal marches?

～

The larger purpose of politics is to attain the good life. But, then, what is the good life? Is it action—participating actively in the good things of life—or is it (ultimately) contemplation—the opportunity and the ability to admire true excellence wherever it occurs? The answers given by ancient democracy (Greece) and modern democracy (as represented by the United States) are significantly different—a difference that arises from how these two peoples and their times view equality. Of course, any society that lays claim to being a democracy must subscribe to equality in certain important areas of life, above all, in political action, which includes the right to speak out in a public forum, the right to vote, and so on. But what about equality in other areas of life? And what is the test of equality? In modern democracy, the test would seem to be active participation. Politics cannot be just a spectator sport. An American citizen has the right to vote in local elections, about which she is knowledgeable, and that would seem to be common sense. But she also has the right to participate in national elections, where her vote counts as much as that of the professor of political science who knows far more about national issues than she, an average citizen, does.

This disregard for the claim of expertise is necessary to political equality. Some Americans have shown, however, a tendency to extend political equality to other areas of endeavor, where its legitimacy is more problematic. Take dancing. Every American has the right to participate in a local dance group for pleasure and to test her talent for dance. But has she the right to join a professional school of the highest caliber if she is not equipped by body shape to do so? The mother of eight-year-old Fredrika Keefer is threatening to sue the San Francisco Ballet for not admitting her daughter. Fredrika is stumpy and lacks the long limbs for patterning to maximum effect, but the city of San Francisco passed a law, sponsored by fat people, forbidding organizations that receive public funds from discriminating on grounds of weight. The case may end up in the California Supreme Court. Should the decision go against the dance company, writes a *New Yorker* (March 5, 2001) reporter, "look to see meatier ballerinas in the future, and may be shorter basketball players as well."

I am led to wonder: Is society able to bear the guilt of undermining my self-esteem when it rules against me on account of my body shape or weight? True, standards will plummet if I am allowed to join the SFB or the NBA, but so what if the result is universal equity—and, let it also be said, universal mediocrity? Populist modern democracy, in my opinion, overvalues action in the estimation of human worth. Ancient democracy did not make this mistake. Although it promoted active engagement in politics and other arenas of life, outstandingly athletics, it also valued—and perhaps it valued even more—spectatorship or contemplation. In both ancient times and our own, the greatest joy in life may not even be performing well oneself; rather, it lies in seeing others, better endowed, perform at the peak of perfection. In endeavors other than politics, to see is also to participate; moreover, to see well is itself a skill that draws on knowledge, and is in no sense passive.

The ancients did not envy as we moderns do. The ultimate reason why they did not was their profound awareness that the greatest excellence could only be contemplated, not enacted or made by mortals, however talented and mighty. And what was this greatest excellence? It was—and I believe it still is—the universe. Before the overwhelming splendor of the universe, we can only be lost in admiration.

Chinese ethnocentrism is well known, but not Chinese racism, a much uglier picture (see Frank Dikötter's, *The Discourse on Race in Modern China*). The two "isms"—the one focusing on culture, the other on physical characteristics—frequently merged in the thought of Chinese officials and intellectuals in the nineteenth and early twentieth centuries. Ethnocentrism meant that the Han Chinese tended to view the non-Han as barbarians, culturally backward and uncouth, but since the words (or characters) used for them commonly bore an animal radical—that of sheep, pig, or snake—the implication was that the barbarians were not just culturally backward but exhibited physical traits that made them not fully human. A common criterion for physical differentiation was skin color. The Chinese saw themselves as white (jade white) and the other peoples as darker skinned, the darkness increasing the further their distance from the center of Chinese civilization: Malays, Indonesians, Indians, and Africans were all considered "black," with Africans the blackest of all. The Chinese first encountered Africans during the ninth century, when Arabs visited coastal cities with their African servants and slaves. By the twelfth and thirteenth centuries, Africans were common enough to be employed by the Chinese as gatekeepers, their facial features and dark skin being judged fearsome enough to ward off evil spirits.

What about Europeans? Well, the Chinese couldn't deny that they were white—but ashen white (the color of death) rather than the jade white that the upper-class Chinese arrogated to themselves. In the nineteenth century, European nations flexed their military muscles and humiliated the Chinese in their own country. One result is that the Chinese increasingly took to describing themselves as yellow—the imperial color—to differentiate themselves sharply from white Europeans. Influential intellectuals, outstandingly Liang Qichao (1873–1929), recognizing reluctantly the proven superiority of whites, sought to ally yellows with whites, and to claim that these were the two superior and progressive races, destined to dominate the earth, unlike browns, reds, and blacks, all of whom were destined to disappear.

Dikötter's book convincingly argues that racism was virulent in modern, nationalistic China. Racism was virulent in the United States and is still a malignant force to be reckoned with. On the other hand, consider the extraordinary gains that have been made. In a Republican administration of the year 2001, the two top diplomats are both black. What job has more social prestige than the ambassadorship to the Court of St. James's or to France? Yet American ambassadors to both countries—and, of course, all other American ambassadors—have to answer to their boss, Secretary of State Colin Powell. Who will help determine American foreign policy—promote Jiang at the expense of Putin, kick ass in Iraq, knock heads in Korea? Not a white male but Condoleezza Rice, an African American woman. Remember that, until fairly recently, diplomacy was the preserve of aristocrats. Even in today's world, the secretary of state exudes far more glamour than does, say, the secretary of labor or transportation. To appreciate how extraordinary this development is, think of Britain, another enlightened country. It just doesn't seem plausible that its foreign secretary will be a Nigerian Briton any time soon.

Russia is a part of the West culturally and politically if only because of its cult of the individual. Consider these examples. The philosopher Nicolas Berdyaev is so much an individualist that he rebels even against the idea of family likeness, which strikes him as a challenge to what he holds dear, "the distinctly individual, the particular in man." Which is more important, love between a man and a woman or the great political movements of our time? Boris Pasternak's answer leaves no doubt. In *Dr. Zhivago*, his heroine, Lara, takes a last look at her dead lover and poet, and says: "The riddle of life, the riddle of death, the beauty of genius, the beauty of loving—that, yes, that we understood. As for such petty trifles as re-shaping the world—these things, no thank you, they are not for us."

The great American poet and democrat Walt Whitman titled his collection of poems *Leaves of Grass*. I wonder what the Russian poet Joseph Brodsky thinks of the title. Uncomprehending and repelled, no doubt. To Brodsky, "grass" is the denial of individuality—of everything that is poetic. Grass, with its prolixity and sameness, is life, not art. Or, as he puts it, "Life itself is defective because it tends to lack the quality of originality. It is too repetitive, too much like grass." Elsewhere he says, "Grass is propaganda" (*Less Than One: Selected Essays*). My last example is the mayor of St. Petersburg, Anatoly Sobchak. He regrets that the Russian language lacks the expression "self-made man." "Faced with a successful individual," Sobchak says in *For a New Russia*, "all we can think to ask is: 'Who backed him? Whose protégé is he?'"

It is baffling to me that Americans, citizens of a great democracy, and strong believers in egalitarianism, should—in their political rhetoric—often refer to themselves as "ordinary,"

"common," or even "little." Stranger still is that this rhetoric is far more likely to come out of the mouth of a liberal (as in "I am for the little people and against the big corporations") than out of the mouth of a conservative. I wonder whether this has to do with the fact that American liberals are often well educated and the fact that many are academics. As academics—as professors in particular—they are used to patronizing the "little people": their students. Liberals in academia also know, through hard experience, that some students will always remain "underdeveloped," no matter how hard they try: they just don't "have it" and so must be taken care of in some patronizing but kindly way. Conservatives, by contrast, pretend to be hard-nosed realists. In fact, lacking (by comparison with liberals) encounters with inequality that are the daily fare of life in academia, they become woolly romantics who eschew the idea (at least in public) of "little people" in constant need of care and feeding. Their rhetoric is that everyone can rise to the top by his or her own initiative and talent, if only Big Brother doesn't put bureaucratic barriers in the way, or demoralize him or her with too little expectation.

Anti-American Americans, many of whom are to be found on college campuses, belong to a tradition of self-denigration that goes back to the French essayist Montaigne in the sixteenth century. He compared the entire human species unfavorably with other animals. In the eighteenth century, reformers ("philosophes") denigrated Western civilization: Europe was a core of darkness surrounded by a rim of light inhabited by sweet South Sea Islanders, sophisticated Persians, and wise Chinese. In subsequent centuries, especially the twentieth, denigration tended to be most bitter when it was directed at one's own country. The technique was to compare self with others. In our time, the superior others may be the marginalized minorities within one's own country—for example, American Indians and African Americans in the United States—and primitive peoples and even extraterrestrials elsewhere. What motivates this need to paint self in such dark colors? One motivation, I suggest, is the pleasure of reverse scapegoating—taking sins upon oneself so that the rest of the world can seem wonderful and pure.

The search for identity and identity politics shows how far the West has strayed from its Christian roots, for, historically, Christianity has promoted the idea that human beings are amphibious, incomplete, hence lacking in any kind of established identity. Unlike other religions, which aim at harmony and peace, Christianity has set up a set of unresolved tensions: "Christ's humanity as against his divinity; man's freedom as against grace and destination; the visible Church as against the invisible Church; the law as against charity; the letter as against spirit; knowledge as against faith; salvation through deeds as against salvation through faith; the State as against the Church; the earth as against heaven; God the Creator as against God the absolute." These tensions, according to Leszek Kolakowski's *Modernity on Endless Trial,* played a major role in the birth of the European Enlightenment, the uniqueness of which—its difference from Asian enlightenments—is its dynamism. The yearning for something fixed—identity—is incompatible with this dynamism. Predictably, in our postmodernist times, both European Enlightenment and Christianity are in bad odor.

Alberto Manguel's *A History of Reading* is about all aspects of reading, including what he calls heroic reading—reading against adverse circumstance. The greatest example of heroic reading, Manguel says, is slaves in the American South: they read despite the threat of physical punishment. My first thought is, How tragically ironic, for the descendants of these heroic readers have lost their passion for reading, to the degree that universities have to seek them out and plead with them to come. Suppose, instead of promoting such popular myths as *Roots* and Kwanza, African Americans had chosen to promote the true story of heroic reading—*their* story? Isn't it just possible that, had that happened, American society would now find that its best schools are black schools, that black faculty are overrepresented in the best universities, and that blacks especially shine in the mathematical and physical sciences, for these were once deemed mere games by white politicians and captains of industry, who, if they attended college, studied law and business?

Another "what if" scenario comes to mind. Suppose Asian immigrants to this country decided that the educational path to success and equality was too difficult: prejudice against Asian students (viewed as children of ignorant laundrymen and cooks) was too strong; moreover, Asians lacked fluency in English. So, reasonably, they turned to politics—the art of using group power—as the fastest route to equality, a route with which they were already familiar, since they practiced it with flair in their own ethnic precincts. The result? Well, no American president dares to have a cabinet without at least two Asian members, the mayor of San Francisco is Chinese, the governor of Virginia is East Indian, the senator from Illinois is Korean, and the Yellow Caucus in Congress is so powerful that no important social policy can pass without its approval. The downside is that Asians are grossly underrepresented in the universities.

A people can choose to lift itself up by politics or by education. The people of Saint Lucia, a banana-exporting island of the Lesser Antilles, opted for education—or, rather, did not allow the infirm gains of politics to overrule the lasting gains of education. Education in the British public-school manner, though imposed by a former colonial power, has been jealously maintained, as the islanders, mostly of mixed African descent, moved gradually to full independence. There was and is no attack on it as a "white" import that has undermined local culture and genius. Literacy rates on the island "hover in the mid-90 percent range, [even though] the per capita income is around $1500, less than one-tenth of the figure in the United States." What an inspiration to poor but aspiring countries the world over that a small, out-of-the way island can produce two Nobel laureates: Sir Arthur Lewis in economics in 1979 and Derek Walcott in literature in

1992 (Howard F. French in the *New York Times*, October 18, 1992).

In an 1884 transcontinental guide called *The Pacific Tourist* is the following gem on the Chinese of San Francisco: "They are great imitators, and so far as known, do they not furnish a striking illustration of the truth of the theory of natural selection? Do not their caudal appendages and power of imitation show their relation to the monkey, and the link they form in the development of the race?"

Well, Americans have come a long way since that time. But perhaps not all the way. In 1999, for example, the Chinese American scientist Wen-ho Lee was accused of having filched missile technology on behalf of China. American politicians, though (interestingly) not American scientists, were incapable of even entertaining the idea that the Chinese could have developed the technology in the course of normal scientific openness and exchange—that is, more or less on their own.

John Osborne, in his play *A Patriot for Me*, used strong language against the Spaniards. "They stink of death. . . . It's in their clothes and their armpits, quite stained with it, and the worst is they're so proud of it, insufferably." This play, written in 1965, could not be given public performance in the United Kingdom because the lord chamberlain objected to certain explicit sexual scenes. Only a decade later, I can imagine it being picketed in the United States by the politically correct, not for the sex but for its crude characterization of a people. Censorship, one way or another, seems inescapable.

I abominate political correctness, only to discover that I can well serve as its poster child. My inability to curse should have given me warning. It's worth remembering that American campuses are temples of middle-class respectability, and this means, among other things, the use of circumlocutions and euphemisms when a more direct and colorful speech is likely to offend. Political correctness has its base in social correctness, which, in addition to inoffensive speech, means having well-off parents, a liberal arts education, and tastefully faded jeans.

An article in *Nature*, reported in the *New York Times* on March 21, 1994, has put a dent in relativism and egalitarianism. Beauty, it would appear, is not in the eye of the beholder, at least not human facial beauty. A study shows that men and women in different cultures consider the same type of female face attractive— large eyes, high cheekbones, and narrow jaw. Art history also suggests that the concept of facial beauty has not changed much in the last few thousand years: even today, the editors of *Vogue* will gladly put Queen Nefertiti on the magazine cover. I am struck by the thought that *égalité* may not be compatible with *fraternité*. If we all have different ideas on beauty, we shan't be able to communicate on this important subject; and without the communication, where is the *fraternité*? On the other hand, if we agree that a hierarchy of beauty exists, we shall have communication and agreement, but *égalité* goes out of the window.

A plumber came to fix my dripping toilet bowl. As he was about to leave he paused to say, "I hope you don't misinterpret my meaning, but, you know, we used to call the problem you had the Chinese water torture." "Yeah," I responded in a mock-superior tone of voice, "We Chinese are kinda subtle in our tortures. You white guys could never go beyond the rack and wheel." With such ethnic stereotyping, we—total strangers— inched toward friendship. We were starting to communicate. Thank God we ignored the PC nannies. If they had their way, the only safe words a white man could use with an ethnic would be "Have a good day!"

We people of the Third World can forgive the West for its imperialism and exploitation. These crude and greedy acts make the West look bad and make us, aggrieved victims, look good. What we cannot forgive—and this is the underlying cause of our deepest resentment—is the West's scientific and technological prowess. If only that too belonged to the past, like imperialism. But no. Astonishing progress continues to be made, and each progress is another welt on our back.

Consider the clock. The National Institute of Standards and Technology is discarding the old clock because it is inaccurate: if an earthling makes an appointment with an extraterrestrial for a conference 3 million years hence, the earthling may be late by as much as ten seconds—a social disgrace. The new atomic clock (adopted in 1993) is still imperfect—it may be off by one second in the year A.D. 3,001,993—but it is an improvement.

Of course, we Third Worlders can always say that we got the whole ball rolling with our initial idea for the sundial or the water clock. But such subterfuge convinces only PC college students. It reminds me of a *New Yorker* cartoon that shows two beavers conversing at the foot of the massive Boulder Dam: the one says to the other, "Well, I didn't actually build it, but it was based on my idea."

The emperor K'ang-hsi (1661–1722) thought that affirmative action, in the name of social justice, could go overboard. He complained: "Shih Shih-lun has complete integrity, but he swung too much in favor of the poor—in any law suit, he favored the commoner against the junior degree holder, and he favored the junior degree holder against the upper gentry. In the same way, Yang Ming-shih insisted on failing the rich examination candidates and pass the poor, even if the latter didn't do as well" (Jonathan D. Spence, *Emperor of China*).

Rembrandt. Who does he think he is? Why should we even now, centuries later, defer to his authority? Well, in cultural

43

studies, a whole industry of belittlement or defacement is in progress. Rembrandt's genius? Call it *Rembrandt's Enterprise!* In reviewing a book of that name, by Svetlana Alpers, Mark Stevens asks in *The New Republic* (August 22, 1988): "What is Alpers's enterprise? She may not know it, but there is a sense in which she is interested in usurping some of Rembrandt's authority. It is the figure of the scholar, one feels, that here asserts cultural primacy. By confining [Rembrandt] to his period and place, he is made a man only of his time, not for all time. As a result, our sense connection with the artists weakens."

The politics of power can be ugly. But is the politics of resentment—the weak's envy of the strong—any prettier?

"Reflecting on Napoleon's comment that no man is a hero to his valet, Hegel remarked that this was true—not, however, because the hero was no hero, but because the valet was a valet," writes John Bayley in *Elegy for Iris.* I don't think we are in danger of becoming a nation of valets, but a small subgroup does run some risk—the subgroup of embittered, college-bred intellectuals who seem driven by resentment and like nothing better than to gossip maliciously about their superiors: big thinkers and artists of the past and scientists of our day.

In the United States, ethnic stereotyping—even when it is favorable—can inflame political passions. Consider the following words: *worship* and *celebration, structure* and *organization, family relations, creativity* and *invention, spirituality.* They are all "good" words; each denotes a human quality or attainment. Yet, as soon as a guy tries to attach an ethnic type to a quality or attainment, all hell can break loose, as Reggie White of the Green Bay Packers found out. What did White, an African American, say? In a speech to the Wisconsin legislature in March 1998, he said blacks are specially adept at "worship and celebration," whites at "structure and organization (and money making)," Hispanics at "family relations," Asians at "creativity and invention," Native

Americans at "spirituality" (University of Wisconsin *Daily Cardinal*, February 3, 2000).

Suppose Reggie White had come up with a different set of couplings. Suppose he told the legislature that blacks excel in "family relations," Asians in "worship and celebration," Hispanics in "structure and organization," Native Americans in "creativity and invention," whites in "spirituality." Would he still be accused of stereotyping? Surely not. If anything, he could be accused of being a contrarian tease. But to think even fleetingly that the second set of couplings is sort of funny is dangerous, for it can only seem so if one has tacitly accepted the original stereotyping as plausible, though obviously nonscientific.

I think the problem lies in the fact that contemporary American society recognizes—although it has never publicly acknowledged—a hierarchy among the different achievements, with "family relations" and "worship and celebration" at the bottom, and "structure and organization" and "creativity and invention" at the top. What is the basis of this ranking? I believe it is the degree that the mind (or intelligence) has to be exercised. "Family relations" are nothing special, since they exist in all human groups; even animals have "family relations." Brainpower is not a prerequisite. As for "worship and celebration," well, they're distinctly human, but somehow there is the feeling that, in these activities, emotion rather than intelligence is more deeply engaged. By comparison, "structure and organization" require planning and forethought—elaborate bureaucratic charts and so on—which suggest the input of an active mind. As for "creativity and invention," there the mind churns away at its peak. One more point is germane to my argument. America, for all the talk about communitarianism, is still highly individualistic. "Family relations" are valued not in themselves, but because good family relations allow members to achieve maximum—guess what?—"creativity and invention."

≈

Gay studies? Students are clamoring for such a program at the University of Wisconsin at Madison. Which cultural and intellectual figures should be included in the curriculum? Confining ourselves to just the modern period, I think the following are a must: poets Walt Whitman and W. H. Auden, novelists Marcel Proust and Thomas Mann, playwrights Tennessee Williams and Jean Genet, film directors Pier Paolo Pasolini and Luchino Visconti, composers Peter Tchaikovsky and Benjamin Britten, mathematicians G. H. Hardy and Alan Turing, philosophers George Santayana and Ludwig Wittgenstein, critical theorists Roland Barthes and Michel Foucault, and geographers Alexander von Humboldt and Derwent Whittlesey.

But apart from sexual preference, these people have nothing in common. They are all, simply, major figures in modern Western civilization. Or is there a subtle gay essence that they all share, giving their works a flavor not to be found in the works of their heterosexual peers? For gay studies to be comparable to ethnic studies, the emphasis will have to be on lifestyles—peculiarities of speech and gesture, manner of dress, culinary art, festivals and parades—rather than on outstanding intellectual and artistic achievements that transcend time and place.

Lifestyle raises the interesting question of choice. One can't choose to be a homosexual; that inclination is deeply embedded in one's nature. But surely lifestyle *is* a matter of choice? Male homosexuals don't have to wear mascara, don't have to show a limp wrist, don't have to address one another by female first names. Or am I wrong here? What's the difference between lifestyle and culture? Is culture fate, or is it also a matter of choice? These are important questions and should be addressed in cultural geography, anthropology, and sociology. But is gay studies, with its narrow focus, the place to do them justice?

Which is politically more daring, a place where there is no private property (a sort of communism), or a place like this?

> Where a father of a boy in the bloom of youth
> Will blame me for doing an injustice.
> "It's a fine thing that you did to my son,

Meeting him all bathed, leaving the gymnasium,
You did not kiss him, speak to him, embrace him,
Or grab his testicles."

That's a question posed by Aristophanes in his play *Birds*. The Greeks were outrageous, weren't they?

Self-confidence and plunder—the taking over of other people's wealth and achievements—predictably go together. The Hsien-pei, a Turco-Mongolian people, are a case in point. After conquering north China, their leaders, in A.D. 494, issued sweeping orders for taking over not only the land and natural resources of the vanquished, but also their culture. In the process, they gave up their own, including even their surnames. Was the result a loss of self-confidence and identity, as modern culturalists argue? No—not at all.

As for the Chinese, from time to time in the nineteenth and twentieth centuries they sought to gain power and self-confidence by taking over such foreign cultural products as modern science and democracy. To the degree that they succeeded, they have freed themselves from the neurotic need to count and polish family heirlooms, even as these continue to be valued as achievements and appropriations (expropriations?) in their own time.

The Greeks want their marbles (the Elgin Marbles) back. The American Indians want their ancestral bones back. The Smithsonian Institution has already returned some of the bones, and the British may eventually return the marbles.

The Greeks want to repossess what they consider to be their heritage—their inspired works of art, their genius. But what if they do not stop there and go on to insist that other ancestral goods also be returned to them—for example, political freedom and democracy, first aired on Greek soil? Would Americans be obliged to pay heavy retroactive royalties for their adaptation and use? American Indians want their bones back because they are sacred objects, the heart of their spirituality. But, then, what about the other Indian spiritual goods appropriated by white Americans without permission, such as reverence for nature? I don't see American Indians demanding *that* heritage back, yet surely a religious worldview is as precious as bones?

One day in 1991, on the television screen, I saw starving Kurdish refugees swarming over the hillsides of Turkey. They were escaping from Saddam Hussein. In the foreground was a little girl riding on her mother's back. Suddenly, my eyes caught sight of something incongruous—a Donald Duck sewn on the child's bib. As suddenly, I recognized that bedraggled crowd thousands of miles away as my neighbors. But how sad and strange to think that it took Donald Duck to persuade me of our common humanity.

Culture, Society, Work

Culture is the product of imagination, and imagination is the ability to see what isn't there. When Michelangelo looks at a block of marble, he is supposed to see a David crying to be let out. This story is meant to illustrate Michelangelo's genius. But even the humblest artisan does the same. He or she looks at formless clay and sees a pot, looks at a tree and sees a log cabin. How else do we make anything at all?

Culture is a kind of error. Some people say 2 + 2 = 3; others say, not so, 2 + 2 = 5. And neither is wholly wrong—out of the ballpark: both are off by just 1. The error is devotedly retained because it makes a people different. In fact, 2 + 2 = 4. Whereas an individual can light on this truth, a collectivity, submerged in its culture and proud of its *difference*, cannot.

Culture, to the extent that it is quaintness and superstition, has rationality as its enemy. Let me illustrate with the emperor T'ai-tsung. An enlightened man, he found many of the beliefs and practices of his time tiresome. One day in the ninth month of the year 628, it happened that some albino magpies built nests in linked pairs on the palace grounds. Officials, believing this association of white birds with paired nests to be auspicious, congratulated the emperor, who, far from being pleased, exclaimed in anger, "I have always laughed at my predecessors' fondness for speaking about auspicious omens. A worthy man is an auspicious omen. How are white magpies beneficial to our affairs?" He thereupon ordered the nests thrown down and the birds released. (See H. J. Weschler in *Offerings of Silk and Jade.*)

The emperor wiped out a quaint belief and replaced it with a rational viewpoint that could be accepted by enlightened individuals anywhere in the world. His rationality deserves cheers—but perhaps only two, for, on the downside, it tends to undermine our lovableness as human beings, which depends on having just these nonrational peculiarities. Look at it this way. No one will throw an affectionate arm around me because I am intelligent. If affection is shown me at all, it is because I am the sort of guy who believes in the auspiciousness of white magpies. Pride in these cultural peculiarities, which are types of error, is stupid. The proper attitude is *affection*—the kind one feels toward adult peccadilloes and the charming mistakes of young children.

Culture is performance. Facial expression, gesture, and social ballet (image and show) permeate our society as they have all others. Moralists see this ubiquitous urge to present the self as a sort of disease, a fall from a state of grace, the loss of some mythic golden age when people were genuine, when they did not put on an act. And yet who said "All the world's a stage"? Shakespeare, not a public relations specialist of our time. The theatrical model of human reality is deeply ingrained in Western thought. And if this model is not as strongly stressed in other societies, it may be because it is taken for granted.

Culture is basically conservative. Once it jells it wants to stay that way. Consider the word *emergency.* Sounds threatening, doesn't it? Yet it is close kin to *emergence.* But why should something that emerges—a gentle image, to my mind—cause an emergency? Panic?

A friend informs me that the word *emergency* took on a negative tone in the seventeenth century when it no longer meant simply "something that emerges" but something that emerges *unexpectedly* and hence is a cause for alarm. Thus John Donne (1631): "The Psalms minister instruction . . . to every man, in every emergency."

One sad result of the weakening of communist secular fervor is the revival of traditional funeral practices in which the ugliest aspects of Chinese culture—superstition and the craving for prestige—are on display. A fairly typical funeral rite among well-to-do urbanites in post-Mao China, reported by an American anthropologist in *Natural History* (December 1988), includes the following rebarbative elements. Son and daughter fight over whether to buy a paper car or a paper bicycle for their deceased mother. The paper car will impress the neighbors more, but it will also deplete the family coffers. The paper bicycle is cheaper, but mother never rode one and would hardly want to try it now in the netherworld. The question of wailing has to be addressed. Would the daughters-in-law, who are known to dislike the deceased, wail with sufficient conviction? The son is supposed to sit by his mother's coffin through the night, but can he do it? He is afraid of ghosts.

If the critical test of whether one likes a culture is whether one approves of its funeral practices, then I have to admit that I am deeply ambivalent about an important aspect of Chinese culture. The crass materialism of Chinese funerals may be explained by the country's lack of a bracing secular philosophy like Stoicism, or of an otherworldly religion, as in certain traditions of Buddhism and Christianity.

~:

The Lakefront Cafe of Memorial Union is being renovated to produce a line of food better suited to the taste of contemporary students. What it used to offer was the traditional fare of the 1930s to 1960s, the fare of my generation. Going down the line, the customer can pick up a green Jell-O salad, Virginia ham and sweet potatoes, apple pie à la mode, and coffee. When the cafeteria reopens in 2002, I expect all that to disappear and to find in its place an international fare of tacos, bean sprouts, hummus, and sushi. Does it matter? I think it does, for food is basic to culture. We are what we eat. Lin Yu-tang put it somewhat differently when he said that "patriotism is the remembrance of the things we have eaten in childhood." So what will become of the American people's sense of self—their patriotism—when the food they are raised on is Mexican one day, Japanese or Middle Eastern the next?

~:

Sometime in Thanksgiving week, I listened to a National Public Radio program on the "music of thanksgiving" throughout the world. It started off with classical Western music—Bach, Handel, Beethoven—and it ended with an American Indian song of praise. The Beethoven was the "Ode to Joy" of the Ninth Symphony. The commentator noted that the Ninth enjoys worldwide popularity and that, indeed, it is more often played in Japan than in the United States, and that whenever a great international occasion demands climactic ceremonial music, it is likely to be the Ninth.

I appreciated what the commentator had to say, for I am devoted to Western classical music myself. Moreover, because the "Ode to Joy" simultaneously warms the cockles of my heart and sends my spirit soaring to the empyrean, I easily assume that it speaks to humanity, that its appeal is universal. Yet how irrational this response is! From a musicological point of view, it is Western classical music that is ethnic and local—the product of a particular people in a particular place and time—whereas the American Indian song of praise, generally deemed ethnic and hence unsuitable as an international grand finale, is in fact universal: its monotone heartbeat thump and air of mournfulness (even in praise) can be found in folk music all over the world.

Are there, then, two kinds of universality? One draws on the rhythmic thumps of the heart. The other draws on these thumps too, but they are barely recognizable as they are woven into the soaring arabesques of mind and spirit.

"A culture is judged by its degree of transparency, by the consciousness it has of itself and others. In this respect the West . . . is still the system of reference." So wrote Maurice Merleau-Ponty in the 1940s. Culture, thus understood, is become problematic by the late twentieth century, because it seems to elevate Western achievement above that of other people. One way to get around the problem is to say that Merleau-Ponty is mistaken, that he has confused culture with intellect. Transparency is the goal of intellect rather than of culture. As for culture, one might almost say that its purpose is obfuscation. It provides people with a comfortable habitat that lets in the sun, but not too much.

Custom that seems natural and virtuous to one people can seem perverse or evil to another. The result is mutual contempt that, under the right conditions, can erupt in murderous conflict. This is a familiar story. What's the cure? One cure is to dethrone custom—that is, to treat even the most sacred practice as manner, as a way of being, worthy of respect but not of passionate devotion. Herodotus, some twenty-five hundred years ago, tried to dethrone custom with the following fable. "Once, while Darius was King, he summoned the Greeks who were at his court and asked them at what price they would be prepared to eat their dead fathers' corpses. They replied that nothing, but absolutely nothing at all, could induce them to do so. Then Darius summoned an Indian people accustomed to eating their fathers, and asked them in the presence of the Greeks at what price they would agree to cremate their deceased fathers. At this the Indians gave loud screams of horror and implored him not even to utter such blasphemy" (III, 38).

In Herodotus's fable, the Greeks and Indians were so enslaved to their practices or *expressions* of piety, which happened to be vastly different, that they completely forgot what they had in common—the *sentiment* of piety.

Here is an example of a type of culture shock that is seldom mentioned in social science literature. It occurs despite good intentions. A woman with red hair and blue eyes enters our courtyard. She wears a Chinese dress and says brightly, "Nie hao ma?" (How are you?). In an instant, a crack opens in the foundation of our world: what we Chinese have always assumed to be human and entirely natural suddenly appears as arbitrary and funny, if not also a little grotesque.

Society, other than hunting-gathering bands, is inevitably stratified. How the lines are drawn varies. Here are two views of how they are or ought to be drawn: that of Henry Timrod, poet laureate of the Confederacy, and that of our contemporary Marxist historian Eric Hobsbawm. In 1861 Timrod saw Southern slavery as "the model of social relations for a new world order in which republican liberty would flourish for the propertied classes and in which security and at least minimal material comfort would be guaranteed to the laboring masses," writes Eugene Genovese in *The Southern Tradition*. And in our own enlightened times? Hobsbawm gave a speech to students of a Central European university in 1993 in which he chose to recognize not the propertied and the laboring classes, as one might expect of a Marxist, but rather two other classes of inequality—the bright and the dull: "What I want to remind you of is something I was

told when I began to teach in a university. 'The people for whom
you are there,' said my own teacher, 'are not the brilliant students
like yourself. They are the average students with boring minds
who get uninteresting degrees . . . and whose examination scripts
all read the same. The first class people will look after themselves, though you will enjoy teaching them. The others are the
ones who need you. Any society worth living in is one designed
for them, not for the rich, the clever, the exceptional'" (*New York
Review of Books*, December 16, 1993).

Right. But a division based on intellect is a great deal more
disturbing than one based on property. One can provide property to those without property, but what can one really do for
"boring minds"?

In November 1999 I was invited to attend a dinner party
given by the Bells in one of their mansions. The Bells are an old
family of wealth and prestige, donors and patrons of the Bell
Museum, the Bell Library, and the Weisman Art Museum of the
University of Minnesota. The dinner was given in honor of the
governing boards of these institutions. I went as one of two out-
of-state guests who were in Minneapolis that day to speak at a
conference sponsored by the Weisman museum. As dinnertime
approached, guests were told to look for their name tags at the
various tables. I peered into the chandeliered dining room but
did not go into it, for I assumed that that was the inner sanctum
for family members and senior trustees of the boards. I did look,
however, at the round tables set up in the large living room, but
couldn't find my name. I moved, finally, to a table in the corridor,
near the kitchen, and there I found it. I should have looked there
first. Why didn't I? Well, I had miscalculated my standing in
society! I was embarrassed and humiliated by this unexpected
reminder of my social presumption. When I wrote *Who Am I?*
I was determined to reveal my weaknesses. But I didn't mention
my sensitivity to social status. I couldn't have. I didn't even know
I was a snob—a social snob, the most despicable kind, in my

opinion—until the Bells enlightened me that November evening.

≈

For society to work, there must be a proper balance of trust and distrust. In a traditional community, trust is built on mutual help among kinsfolk and neighbors, all close by. Distrust is built into the system as well. Behind partially drawn curtains, neighbors—vigilant Little Brothers—keep a watchful eye.

In our huge impersonal society, trust—not dependent on propinquity—is more important than ever. I became aware of this several years ago when I at last sought the help of a financial adviser so that my savings can increase at a sturdier rate. He soon asked me to sign a sheaf of (to me) utterly incomprehensible forms. I wondered a bit whether I was signing away not only my savings but also my freedom, my life. Just a bit. For the fact is, I trusted him. Trust in strangers—that's how modern society works. But there must also be distrust; hence, the existence of suspicious lawyers and police, watchdog committees and investigative journalists. Nevertheless, in human relationships, what chiefly distinguishes modern from traditional society is modern society's far greater dependence on trust. As civilization advances, its people become more trustful—more innocent and childlike—out of necessity.

≈

Is the fudging of boundaries a trend in modern and postmodern society? The fudging of spatial boundaries is well known to geographers. In premodern times, city, countryside, and wilderness were sharply bounded. People couldn't help knowing they were in the city when they entered the monumental gate. They also knew what it was like to be in the heath, as distinct from being in the countryside, where the king's writ— that is, cosmic order—still held. (See Shakespeare's *King Lear.*) As for the fudging of temporal boundaries, consider marriage. In the old days, marriage was a boundary event of great import. All the delays and postponements—the hand holding and kissing but nothing more—and the drama of the wedding ceremony itself were meant to emphasize the criticality of a particular moment. No more! Not in our age of gradualism and provisional commitments. The phenomenon of birth offers another example. What has happened to the grand entrance? "It's a boy!" the nurse announced with theatrical flair. Well, we now can know "it's a boy"—and a lot of other things about him, too—long before his birth. As for education, when does it end and work life begin? Fifty years ago, it was high school graduation. Now it is college graduation. Or has that event also lost its luster because it is merely a pause before graduate school? Even death has lost its edge. Dying, thanks to modern science, promises to be an interminable process. We need the legal device of a living will to ensure that at some point the plug is pulled and we finally die.

In a good society, most things actually work: drop a postcard into a mailbox and it will eventually wend its way to the other side of the globe. But it must not work *too* well if it is to remain good. There must be room for a little chaos, which in archaic Greek means *gap* rather than *disorder.* More precisely, the ancients understood chaos to be the gap formed when heaven was pried apart from the earth and through it Kronos, the Titans, Zeus, and in time all sorts of creatures emerged. In other words, no chaos, no creativity, no life. A perfectly ordered society—one in which everything fitted (as sky and earth once fitted) and everything worked—would be a dead society.

Am I pleased or annoyed when my behavior can be understood or explained by some social-scientific hypothesis? I can't quite make up my mind. To be sure, I am pleased to be part of the human race, to have the peaceful anonymity of being a textbook example. On the other hand, I know that this is a kind of death wish. From time to time, at least, one ought to be glad to be an unexplained residual. This ornery posture is more than an egoistical desire to be unique. At stake is this important moral question: How can one have respect for others—how can one even see them—if they all toe the regression line?

Brazilian dockworkers went on strike in 1960 for "shame pay" when they had to unload new toilets (*Time*, August 30, 1963). The implications are embarrassing. How can we professors ask for pay at all when we unload Truth, Beauty, and Goodness?

Even in the rich Western world, some jobs are terrible. One of the worst is employment in a pet food factory in California. Workers there sweat to produce pet food that is "embalmed garbage in high-price cans," says Theodore Roszak in *Person/Planet*. How does it feel to get up at five in the morning, fight through traffic, check into the factory to be thoroughly bored and disgusted for the next eight hours, all to gorge the fat cats of the leisured class?

A far better job is collecting flower petals at Grasse, France, to make perfume. At night, under the glow of lanterns, men, women, and children pick the dew-covered petals, put them in burlap sacks, and sell them to farmers who sell them to merchants. The poetry is there, just a bit spoiled by the thought that the product's final destination is the armpits of the world's pampered class.

The most bizarre job I know of is producing "the money shot" (ejaculation for pay) in the San Fernando Valley's porn industry. It is a job in which the men can really strut their stuff. Unfortunately, a hard-on (*wood* is the industry's term) cannot be delivered on command. Moreover, failure is for all to see. While the male star desperately manipulates his soft member, his female partner earns her pay by just lying naked on the couch. It doesn't help him to know that the technicians, too, are watching with growing impatience and disdain.

Toy making. Now, that's an appealing job. Engaged every day in making children happy, toy makers are probably happy themselves; and happy people are generally good people, in my opinion. I think of young George Willig, a designer for the Ideal Toy Corporation. He has an unusual hobby: climbing the slick face of skyscrapers. On May 26, 1977, he climbed all the way to the top of the World Trade Center in New York and became an instant hero. He explained to reporters that he had originally planned to scale the tower a day earlier, but couldn't because he had made an appointment to give blood. "I couldn't go on making excuses. So I arbitrarily picked today." That's quite a life, isn't it? Giving blood to the sick or happiness to the young, as required, and then, in one's spare time, demonstrating to the world the freedom and extraordinary daring of the human spirit.

Workers historically have taken pride in what they make: cheese, furniture, highways, motorcars, and so on. Their pride is in the objects that they have introduced into the world. The last thing they want is to draw attention to themselves—their body, skills, and charms—for that would remind them of what prostitutes do. We now see why a feeling of unease can descend on a local people when they realize that cultural-ethnic tourism has become their economic mainstay. In order to continue to prosper, they have to sell their smile, their accent, their heritage, their grandma rather than what they make. They are no longer workers but charmers.

Home, Rootedness, Place

"Home is the place where, when you have to go there, they have to take you in," Robert Frost wrote. This is a cry of despair, for who would want to go to a place that has to take you in? Heaven does not have to take me in. God cannot be coerced. On the other hand, if I am bad enough, Hell has no choice but to accept me, just as on earth, the city jail must accept me when I have bashed a policeman on the head.

In the famous Bible story, the prodigal son returned to his
father's welcoming arms. He counted on being accepted, if not
quite on such generous terms. André Gide, author and homosexual rebel who felt deeply ambivalent about home, gave a
twist to the story. In his version, the prodigal son returned to the
bosom of his family, but with a sense of defeat; and so when his
younger brother in his turn wanted to leave home, his last words
to him were: "Allons! Embrasse-moi, mon jeune frère: tu emportes
tous mes espoirs. Soi fort; oublie-nous. Puisse-tu ne pas revenir."
("Let's go! Give me a hug, kid. You carry all my hope. Be strong,
forget us. May you never return." From *The Return of the Prodigal
Son*.)

A rootless cosmopolite who left China at age ten, I wonder
what authentic feelings of nostalgia toward the land of my birth
I still have. Not for food, which usually provides the firmest anchorage to childhood and the past, perhaps because good Chinese food is readily obtainable in the United States. If not food,
then what? I come up with three categories of experience: landscape, music, and social relations.

As the train glided through the Canadian Rockies, I glanced
out of the window and saw a Chinese painting of towering peaks
wrapped in mist, trees with twisted limbs, waterfalls, winding
roads, and rapid-flowing streams. Only a grass hut with contem-
plating hermit was missing. I thought: "My native landscape is
one of verticals and horizontals, peaks and flat alluvial plains. So
what am I doing living in a Midwestern American landscape of
rolling hills and dales, red barns and cows?"

Without doubt, the music that elevates my spirit is Western
classical music. And yet my soul music—using *soul* in the African
American sense—is Chinese: specifically, Peking opera. Arias
from the Peking opera are part of my Chinese childhood. On the
rare occasions when I hear them now, I feel the blood of my ancestors stir anew through my veins, and I shudder.

I am nostalgic for what I remember as the informality of
Chinese entertaining. After dinner, while guests gather around

to chat or play mah-jongg, the hostess nonchalantly says, "I am sleepy. I am going upstairs to rest. Do stay and enjoy yourselves."

On my way home, I do not feel that this goal—home—lies in my future. On the contrary, I feel I am moving back in space and time. Home connotes the past for a number of reasons. It is the familiar world, and familiarity implies the passage of time, a lengthening past. Home is also often considered the center of one's life; and center, insofar as it connotes origin, is the point from which one moves out to the world and the future, and so cannot itself be the future. Home is the place we come from and return to, rather than just go to. As a child learning English, I was struck by the asymmetry between "going to school" or any other place and "going home." I wanted to know what happened to the *to*.

When I see a story by Isaac Bashevis Singer I usually skip it. Having read an interview with Singer (in *Conversations with IBS*), I now know why. Singer is committed to roots and the particular. He has little sympathy for writers who, for lack of grounding in place, write thin, crystalline stories that strive to convey some larger view. Singer himself, though he has lived in America for fifty years, still writes in Yiddish. His stories are still often located in the Warsaw of his youth. He despises assimilationists. Arthur Koestler, because he tried hard to assimilate, "fails both as a man of dignity and as a writer" (Singer's words). The interviewer asks Singer, "If you had fallen in love with a non-Jewish woman, could you possibly have married her?" Singer's answer: "I don't know." So much for the power of passion to leap over ethnic walls.

By contrast, consider another esteemed writer, Marguerite Yourcenar. She is of bourgeois background, yet blessed with a father who is sufficiently unorthodox to say to his daughter, "Where is one better off than in the bosom of one's family? Anywhere." Also, "A man is only at home when he is away."

Yourcenar herself is footloose. Her suitcase is, so to speak, always packed. She is willing to live anywhere. But what about her work? Doesn't it have to be rooted in personal experience? Well, her most famous and esteemed book, *Memoirs of Hadrian*, is about the politics, the military strategy, the intimate thoughts and passions of a great Roman emperor. Experience and circumstance more different from the author's can hardly be imagined. The book, I might add, was completed on the Santa Fe train as it rushed clickety-clack into the New Mexico desert.

I offer two more observations. Singer's technique entails the minute description of external behavior. He disdains authors who tell you what the characters think. By contrast, Yourcenar, in *Memoirs of Hadrian*, is centrally engaged with what goes on in Hadrian's head. Being rooted means anchorage in the externalities of life; being rootless means that, if one is to have any sort of anchorage at all, it would have to be in one's own thoughts. Another point to note is this: Singer's stories deal exclusively with heterosexual love, and with it, necessary ties to kin, community, and place. Yourcenar, by contrast, shows an unusual interest in the homoerotic, starting with Hadrian's affair with young Antinous. Homoerotic love, with no procreational consequence and responsibility, tends to be placeless; it has no place for heirlooms and real estate.

When did I first realize that I could be at home in the United States? Answer: around six o'clock one morning in 1955, at a bus rest stop. As a student I traveled all over the country by Greyhound, being too poor to travel by other means. Moreover, I wanted not only to see America, but also to rub shoulders with her humbler folks. One could do that in a packed Greyhound bus, especially at night, after many long hours on the road. In the darkness of night, passengers, tired of talking or reading, dozed and slumped into one another to form gently heaving lumps of common humanity. And so we remained mile after mile in the partial oblivion of restless sleep, until we felt a sudden swerve in the motion of the bus. It stopped to the shushing sound of pneumatic brakes. The driver shouted, "Breakfast stop!" We stumbled out and filed into a neon-lit cafeteria. I sat on a stool and ate a hearty meal of eggs sunny side up, toast, and hash browns washed down with coffee. We still had a few minutes left. I stepped into the cool air. We happened to be somewhere in Southern California. Palm trees stood out ink-black against a brightening horizon. I looked at the stark landscape, savored the bit of marmalade lodged between my teeth, smelled the desert air faintly imbued with the odor of gas fumes, breathed deeply, and felt glad to be alive. Yes, I thought, I could make a home here.

I became a naturalized citizen in 1973. In 1975, after one year as a Fulbright scholar in Australia, I returned to the United States. At Customs, I lined up behind the sign that said "Citizens" for the first time. As I shuffled toward the booth, I wondered whether the immigration officer would recognize my new status. He did. He glanced at my passport and said, "Welcome home." In case I should sound too naively pleased, let me refer you to Vladimir Nabokov, a sophisticated European if there ever was one. Even he confessed to feeling a tinge of pleasure and pride when he whipped out his U.S. passport at the crossing of the borders. It had less to do with power than with the big open sky over Montana.

The USA-Iranian soccer match in Los Angeles in the fall of 1999 was touted in the news media as possibly the beginning of a thaw in U.S.-Iranian relations, somewhat along the lines of the Ping-Pong match, then thaw, between the United States and China years earlier. I was struck by the event for another reason. It raised for me troubling questions of loyalty and attachment. The stadium was packed with some 50,000 predominantly Iranian American spectators. They waved mostly Iranian flags and cheered the Iranian team. The sports commentator sounded unsure as to how he should label them. Were they Iranian Ameri-

can? American? Or—given the object of their passionate loyalty—Iranian?

The crowd was made up of immigrants, but also second-gen-
eration youngsters who knew no other native land than, say,
California or Oregon, youngsters who could one day be elected
president of the United States. I was led to reflect on my own ultimate loyalty: "Here I am. I have lived in the United States for
half a century, as against only ten years in China. I have taught
and nurtured generations of American students, corrected their
papers, boosted their morale, wiped their noses and combed
their hair, so to speak. My closest friends (with a couple of exceptions) are non-Chinese. I have publicly and proudly claimed
to be a cosmopolite who shrinks in distaste from slogans that
draw on ties of blood and soil. Though my native tongue is
Chinese, I now even dream in American English. With all these
personal, cultural, and sentimental ties to my adopted land, do
I know which team I would cheer in a soccer match between the
United States and China? Will *cri du sang* take over?"

What worries me in the larger context is this: If even a shallow person who lives almost entirely in his head (like me) remains vulnerable to visceral passion, what about people less
shallow—the vast majority of the world's population? Is it any
wonder that ethnic partisanship and violence can erupt in countries that at one time seem sophisticated and cosmopolitan?

Some characteristically American good places have disappeared from the street scene in my lifetime. One is the drugstore. In its heyday (from the 1930s to the mid-1960s) it was a
microcosm that had just about everything a needy human being
could reasonably want. This was undeniably true of the campus
Rexall I patronized in Albuquerque from 1959 to 1965. Fractured
a leg bone? On the drugstore walls, next to college pennants
and photos of football greats, was an assortment of crutches.
Hungry? Try a double cheeseburger. Indigestion? Complaint
would elicit, free of charge, an Alka-Seltzer pill and a glass of
water. Food for thought? Try the *Atlantic Monthly*, Salinger, or

Hesse. Lonely? Booths provided padded seats for teenage smooching. The old, for their part, could perch on stools at the counter and have their loneliness eased by the soda jerk's friendly patter on the weather or the latest baseball score.

I am reluctant to admit that mere physical environment can affect my mood. Samuel Johnson (1709–84) was likewise reluctant. "Change of place" shouldn't make much difference, for the true source of happiness or misery lies in ourselves, he opined. But then he remembered who said "The mind is its own place, and in itself / Can make a heaven of hell, a hell of heaven." It was Satan—the fallen but still defiant archangel in Milton's *Paradise Lost.*

When modern cities look so much alike, their only difference may be the street names and the language that signs and advertisements are written in. In *Christopher and His Kind* (1976), Christopher Isherwood describes how he looked about his room in Berlin, at the courtyard outside with its puddles of water, at a patch of the sky between tenement houses. He could be anywhere. Both architecture and nature seemed international, placeless, until his eyes suddenly lit on a poem engraved on one of the courtyard walls:

> Seele des Menschen
> Wie gleichst du dem Wasser!
> Schicksal des Menschen,
> Wie gleichst du dem Wind!

Germany, of course. Indeed, how unmistakably German the place—even the sky—suddenly seemed.

When I see slides taken by friends during a vacation or a field trip, I often say to myself "That's a place I want to visit" but almost never "That's a place I want to live in." Is the failure to evoke habitability inherent to pictorial presentation, or just to presentation of not the highest quality? It's just possible that a Constable landscape or a Vermeer interior will persuade me to say "That feels like home. I wouldn't mind living there."

Eighty-year-old Bernard Berenson, the famed scholar of Renaissance art, claimed to live in a smelly crumbling hut with thinly thatched roof and bad drains, although young admirers who visited him were under the impression that he was domiciled in a beautiful Italian villa. Berenson was, of course, referring to his body. Young people forget that they themselves live, first of all, in their comely, well-built, fully functioning bodies. No wonder they don't much mind the sagging porch and clogged drains of their apartment building.

Is the ultimate good place more like a palace or more like a garden? Consider Buddha's answer. According to him, there are five levels of existence. Lowest is hell—a pit of hot charcoal for the unredeemable. Next is a cesspool for beings enslaved by animality. As spirit makes its home in animate bodies, existence is like "coming under a tree in a desert, but with sparse leaves and little shade." At its best, human life may be compared to sitting under "a tree growing on even ground, with dense leaves and foliage giving thick shade." Best of all is the deva world of divinity, which is like a palace.

Like a palace? Why would someone as unworldly as Buddha envisage the palace as the ultimate good place? Didn't he escape his father's palace when, as a young man, he sought enlightenment?

In a class titled "Environment and the Quality of Life," I draw attention to a widely accepted view of the good life, captured by

Ferdinand when he utters his hope for "quiet days, fair issue and long life," and by Juno when she speaks approvingly of "honor, riches, marriage blessing / Long continuance, and increasing" in Shakespeare's *Tempest.* The Chinese endorse this view whole-heartedly. In shops, restaurants, and the humbler homes, one frequently encounters three characters: *shou* (long life), *fu* (luck, prosperity), and *lu* (emoluments and happiness).

Fine, I say to the class. But something is missing from this sensible view, and what is missing is achievement—the idea of excellence. I then turn to another view of the good life. To capture students' attention, I describe it, with a touch of hyperbole, as paradisiacal. What place do I have in mind? The university, I say, and I can see that my reply disappoints and disconcerts some students. Yet why not? What, after all, are the characteristics of paradise? It is blessed by eternal youth, and that's what I find at the university. In my forty years of teaching, I have changed from personable young man to wrinkled curmudgeon, while across the floor, ten feet from me, tauntingly year after year, are the blooming faces of youth. Second, paradise must have a beautiful environment. This is important. Plato's school was located in a garden. Monasteries and monastic schools often sought to establish themselves in places of natural beauty. Bernard of Clairvaux (1090–1153) located his houses in the midst of natural loveliness to encourage spiritual devotion. American seminaries, colleges, and universities were conceived as paradises, cordoned off from the corrupting influence of cities by belts of wilderness.

I have used the word *paradise* rather than *Eden,* for Eden is all nature, prior to knowledge, a soft, dewy place of animal innocence. Places of learning are clearly different. Athenian youths had a handsome school to themselves, but rather than lead lives of ease, they toughened their bodies with wrestling and their minds with geometry. Monasteries might boast natural and architectural beauty, but monks lived in cells and ate spartan meals. As for the University of Wisconsin at Madison, for all its luxuriance of tree-lined walks, sunlit lawns, and amply stocked libraries, the students themselves are housed in warrenlike dorms and survive on pizza. Paradise cannot just be a place of sensual indulgence, if only because human nature would quickly deteriorate. In any case, whatever happens in heaven, on earth the good place cannot be an end in itself. It must have a purpose, and what can that be other than schooling for moral and intellectual excellence?

Human Ties and Isolation

Modern novelists, unlike Tolstoy, tend to avoid depicting good people and happy events. Historians may be likewise faulted. They should heed what Saint Paul has to say in his letter to the Philippians (4:8): "Whatsoever things are true, whatsoever things are honest, whatsoever things are just, whatsoever things are lovely, whatsoever things are of good report, if there be any virtue, if there be any praise, *think on these things* " (I added the emphasis). How rarely we intellectuals think on these things. The fear of being thought naive so often lands us in excessive negativity and falsehood.

Husband and wife, in the John Updike novel *Roger's Version*, have grown indifferent to each other. They chat listlessly. The wife looks out of the living room window and says, "Why don't I what? I was spying on the Kriegmans, envying them their happiness." The husband replies: "That's the way we look to them, too. Don't worry about it. All families look great through windows."

A bit cynical perhaps? Marital bliss—domestic bliss—is real and not just a fenestral illusion. My authority is Virginia Woolf, who can hardly be accused of excessive sentimentality. In her diary, she notes the happiness of her friends the Leafs: "Why all this pother about life? It can produce old Walter, bubbling & chubby; and old Lotta, stately and content; and handsome Charles, loving & affectionate. Plunge deep into Walter's life and it is all sound and satisfactory. His son kisses him and says,

'Bless you father.' He sinks back chuckling on his cushions. He chooses a macaroon. He tells a story. Lotta purrs, in her black velvet dress."

Poor Virginia Woolf. She was the outsider, a family friend who occasionally looked in: "Only I am exiled from this profound natural happiness. That is what I always feel; or often feel now—natural happiness is what I lack, in profusion."

Here is another example of natural happiness, observed this time by me. The location is the Starbucks coffee shop on State Street in Madison; the time about ten one Saturday morning in late December. Most students have gone home for the Christmas holidays. There are, however, two youngsters—a boy and a girl—sitting within finger-touching distance at a small table. The boy is saying excitedly to the girl, "My brother and I told our parents that we were going on a walking tour of Mexico during spring break. What we intended all along was to head straight to Tijuana for our first testosterone-driven orgy! We stopped by home before returning to Madison. That evening, we all sat around watching TV. Suddenly, on the screen, was a shot of my brother and me, bare-chested, shouting inanities and swilling beer! It was a special on college high jinks! Our poor parents were stunned. But so were we, for we had no idea that we were on camera. Then we all burst out laughing and slapped each other on the back."

Same location—Starbucks. A father walked in with his small son in a stroller, which he parked next to a table while he went to the counter for coffee. He returned to the table, bent over the stroller, and politely inquired, "Sir, is this table taken?" The performance couldn't be for other clients, for I was the only one in the coffee shop, and it certainly wasn't for me. And it wasn't really for his child, who was too young to understand. So what was it? Paternal pride, pure and simple. I felt privileged to be a witness. But I was also saddened, like Virginia Woolf, to be only a witness.

Same location—Starbucks. I sit next to the Korean woman who is a regular client—indeed, she practically lives there. Her most conspicuous trait is that she carries on a lively conversation with herself, her hand chopping the air to make a point or slapping her lap in appreciation of a really clever joke. "Home entertainment," I say to myself, "but one that can lead to madness." Yet, on second thought, what is it that I do at Starbucks besides sipping coffee? I too carry on a lively conversation with myself, the only difference being that I tamp down my physical gestures, remaining silent and appreciating my own little witticisms with the barest hint of a smile.

The university's Memorial Union is packed with people on weekends—students, of course, but also young children, many of whom belong to the older students. One such student walks down the hallway with his son, who looks about six years old. They are holding hands. Suddenly, the boy breaks away, dashes into an arcade full of video games, and shouts excitedly, "Dad, what a great school you are at!" But dad is too distracted to appreciate what his child is saying. A stranger—me—smiles. The boy has made my day.

Alfred North Whitehead wrote to his son North on December 10, 1924. After first saying that he can imagine his grandchildren growing up by predictable stages, he adds that, looking back on life, he considers bringing up a family "by far the achievement most worth while." I find this conclusion rather surprising in one of the world's greatest mathematician-philosophers, known for his total engagement with his esoteric subject, his seeming unawareness of the routines and rhythms of the people around him. In the letter, Whitehead notes that much of life is recollection, and what one most fondly recollects are the intimate (though often also anxious) moments of parenthood. These moments relieve life of "a sense of barrenness which I have often noticed damping elderly people who have never [known them]." (Victor Lowe, *Alfred North Whitehead*)

Mary McCarthy's future husband (James West) went back to Switzerland to visit with his young children. Once he was there, he lined them up and clipped their toenails. That's intimacy—so rare in fatherhood until our time. Mothers, of course, have always had intimate jobs, beginning with nursing. No male can imagine what it is like to have a small mouth tugging at his breast. Women have it good. As for the unmarried, what is there for them to recollect in old age?

Bob Dylan reached a peak of popularity as singer in the 1960s and 1970s, especially in Minneapolis, where he could be seen discussing politics with Hubert Humphrey in a drugstore near the University of Minnesota campus. I bought a recording of his, my only nonclasssical record, out of curiosity. I was struck by this male singer crooning tenderly, over and over again, "my blue-eyed son" and "my darling young one" in the song "A Hard Rain's A-Gonna Fall." How wonderful to be able to use these words, I thought twenty-five years ago. I heard the song again in 1994, at the Espresso Royale, on Madison's State Street. The words, still wonderful to my ears, reveal deep happiness. I know that, but it now occurs to me that they also reveal privilege. Take "darling." When I see a cute baby or toddler, I have the right to say to his parent, "What a darling child!" But I do not have the right to call the child—nor, in the absence of the appropriate degree of intimacy, anyone else—"darling." If you think this a minor deprivation, think again.

70

"What a happiness it was for me to have such a brother!—a brother who, moreover, loved me passionately," wrote the Russian geographer Peter Kropotkin (1842–1921). When Peter was sixteen years old and a trainee in the Imperial School for Pages, his brother, Alexander, one year older, was a cadet in a military college. They could rarely meet. One night, Alexander escaped from his barricaded college, walked five miles through fields and rough roads terrorized by wild dogs in the hope that he could see Peter briefly in their Moscow home. (If Alexander had been caught, the corporal punishment would have been severe enough to send him to the hospital.) The family serfs conspired with the two brothers and hid them in the coachmen's house. "They looked at us," Peter Kropotkin recalled in his *Memoirs* (1899), "and took seats at a distance, along the walls, exchanging words in a subdued tone, so as not to disturb us; while we two, in each other's arms, sat there till midnight, talking about nebulae and Laplace's hypothesis, the structure of matter, the struggles of the papacy under Boniface VIII with the imperial power, and so on."

What a charming story. I don't believe it can be topped. Human beings are shown at their best—loving, loyal, courageous, and intellectual.

You see or hear something that makes you breathless with joy and yearn for home, which you know is not of this world. You tell this to a friend who nods in sympathy but then tells you that quite something else—another image, sound, or smell—makes *him* breathless with joy and yearn for home. You share. But then again, you don't. Is this bad? No. Not if you believe in a God whose store of goodness is so vast and varied that, understandably, each limited human creature can respond only to a small token. But that small token is enough to lead you and your friend, along different paths, to the common, yearned-for destination—God.

A young woman with a shaved head is paraded through the Parisian streets. Her mother explains to the journalist Malcolm Muggeridge what has happened. A German soldier was billeted with them. He turned out to be very friendly and helped them with food and fuel supplies. Almost inevitably, the soldier and the girl fell in love. The girl became pregnant. When the German troops moved out, the soldier stayed behind to be with her. Members of the French Resistance, among whom was the girl's brother, eventually caught the soldier and shot him. They then shaved the girl's head to mark her as a traitress. Muggeridge comments, in *Confessions of a Twentieth-Century Pilgrim*, "What is remarkable is that her love for her lost lover, and joy in the child she will bear him, swallows up her suffering and grief. That is to say, she is Liberated."

Is this another version of the Romeo-and-Juliet story? The Capulets (France) and the Montagues (Germany) are traditional enemies, reconciled fleetingly in the entwinement of young flesh. Where friendship is out of the question and mutual respect is fragile, lust from which genuine love can grow may be the answer.

When I travel I prefer to check into a motel rather than stay with friends. I used to think that the reason is fatigue: after long hours on the road and a long sociable dinner, I yearn for the mindless comfort that only television in a motel room can provide. But there may be a deeper reason. In a friend's house, when I withdraw into the bedroom I do not find that I have left the social world behind. On the contrary, the conversation with my host continues via the room and its objects. What is the provenance of the porcelain pineapple on the mantelpiece? And this book about Antarctica on the bedside table. I have not known that my friend has a yen for polar exploration. Or does the book belong to his son? It is not that I seek to know. Quite the contrary. I seek sleep—blissful oblivion. But the strong personality of the room keeps me awake and makes me uncomfortably aware that the mutual understanding established so recently in the living room may be an illusion.

Einstein is one of the world's great individualists. Even the marching band is to him an aberration. How can sane people want to march in lockstep? His advice to the new Ph.D. is to spend the next two years alone in a lighthouse and think. And yet one of the most eloquent evocations of the "we" comes from Einstein. In 1952, at the grave of a physicist friend, he says:

> Brief is this existence, as a fleeting visit in a strange house. The path to be pursued is poorly lit by a flickering consciousness, the center of which is the limiting and separating "I." The limitation to the "I" is for the likes of our nature unthinkable, considering both our naked existence and our deeper feeling for life. The "I" leads to the "Thou" and to the "We"—a step which alone makes us what we are. And yet the bridge which leads from the "I" to the "Thou" is subtle and uncertain, as is life's entire adventure. (Einstein papers, Boston)

The most successful examples of community life are inorganic—rock, planet, star—according to Alfred North Whitehead. His criteria for success are stability and perfect communication. From the inorganic peak, the less successful communities are, successively: plant-and-animal, traditional human, and modern human. The more the members of a community are self-aware, each (moreover) able to acquire a distinctive worldview that is subject to change, the less likely they are to have things in common and the rarer the occasions of mutual understanding, though when they do occur they can be profoundly satisfying.

Instability in the modern community means that it can break down and revert to the simpler and more stable condition of the traditional community. The traditional human community, for its

part, is inclined to revert to the still greater simplicity of a biological community, and biological community to mineral community, where communication is direct, with no possibility of
misunderstanding. And doesn't that sound restful? Aren't we all a
bit tempted? (See Victor Lowe, *Alfred North Whitehead*.)

Pope John Paul I died unexpectedly on September 28, 1978,
after serving as pontiff for only thirty-three days. He died alone,
without receiving the last rites. Conspiracy theories about what
happened abound, but John Cornwell—who wrote a book, *A
Thief in the Night*, on the subject—concludes that there was no
conspiracy, that the pope "died of neglect" and "lack of care."
How can that be? It can be, for great power isolates the good as
well as the bad.

A nine-year-old boy who lost both arms in a composting
machine on his dad's farm in Georgia had been trying not to cry,
a local newspaper reported. "I think he's been taking it pretty
good," his father said. "Oh, a time or two he's said, 'Daddy, I
want to hug you, but I can't 'cause I ain't got no arms,' and his
eyes would tear up."

How dramatically modern technology can bring two human
beings together in a moment of need is illustrated in the following story, related by David Breashears in *High Exposure*. Rob Hall
was a professional mountain climber. In May 1996 he tried to
lead a group of amateurs to the summit of Mount Everest and
failed. Several died. Rob used the little energy he had left to
make a last, desperate attempt to save one of his charges. He
failed in that too, with the result that he was stranded on a narrow ledge a few hundred feet below the peak. He radioed for
help. Several rescue teams were dispatched. All had to turn back
as the weather deteriorated. Miraculously, Rob lived through the

night. He must have known that he couldn't survive another night. He didn't. But he did not die alone, for before he drew his last breaths, he spoke by satellite radio with his wife in New Zealand at the other end of the globe. She was about to give birth to their first child. "Hi, sweetheart," he said. "Are you warm, my darling?" she asked. Eventually, Rob had to sign off. "I love you. Sleep well, my sweetheart. Please don't worry too much."

André Gide said that when he narrated a story at a social gathering, he always tended to rush the ending for lack of confidence that he could hold his listeners' attention. And yet he had a way with words. He was, after all, a Nobel laureate in literature. Why this lack of confidence? Well, experience told Gide that when he was interrupted in the middle of a story, no one ever asked him later, "What happened next?"

Death is the interruption of a life story. Regrettable, but who really wants to know what could have happened next? We are all far too busy composing our own life stories.

When pedagogues commend "participation," they seem to have in mind not a quiet class in which students listen, but rather a noisy class in which they speak out, interrupting one another and the teacher. Yet one certainly participates by listening, and it may well be the more demanding way. Think of monkeys in a tropical forest. They speak out—*do* they speak out! But do they ever listen? Is it even within their intellectual capacity to listen? We human beings occasionally listen, and when we do we recognize the individuality and worth of another. And what is the worth? In large part, it is his or her take on the world. So shut up and listen.

In true listening, one mind is penetrated, ravished by another—a degree of intimacy rarely achieved in copulation.

Maybe that's the problem: we don't want that degree of intimacy, we don't want to be penetrated and ravished.

"You see one hippopotamus and you have seen them all." To the extent that this is true, it explains why hippopotami are never lonely or neurotic. A hippo lives in the assurance that it is representative of its species. Anatomically, one individual is much like another. Moreover, what one hippo can know is little different from what the species, collectively, can know. In the sharpest contrast are human beings. Anatomically, one human being is much like another. But what one human being knows is at best only a tiny fraction of the vast knowledge accumulated by the species. My understanding of the world, for example, is based in large part on the five thousand books I have read. But the Library of Congress contained, in 1981, 6.3 *million* books in the English language alone. In my desperate need for community, for the assurance that what I know is pretty much what my neighbors know, I have wished at times that only five thousand books had been written—or better, none at all!

For his last appearance as music director of the Minnesota Orchestra, Maestro Stanislaw Skrowaczewski chose two all-time favorites: Tchaikovsky's Symphony no. 6 (the *Pathétique*) and Stravinsky's *The Rite of Spring.* The performance of the *Pathétique* was superb. The last two dying notes were plucked in the midst of total silence. During the intermission, young couples holding hands strolled along the reflecting pool of Peavey Plaza. The moon shone through the haze of the balmy evening. It was a romantic scene, and also somewhat sad as I gazed upon it from behind glass doors and thought that Tchaikovsky himself knew nothing of moonlit strolls with a beloved. And how would he have taken that paean to heterosexual passion and fertility, *The Rite of Spring?*

"We" implies "they." Their repetitive use, setting the one against the other, promotes communal warmth and solidarity. By contrast, "I" implies other "I"s—all other human beings who can also say "I." "I" thus points to universality, to a world of equal "I"s, and to cool communities of specialized interests. Another difference is this. "We," as in the royal or editorial "we," is a claim to authority: what "we" think or say must be true. By contrast, using the first person singular is a claim to only one individual's view. Yet the result need not be solipsism and subjectivity. On the contrary, in an atmosphere of tolerance, in the recognition of the strength and weakness of the views of other "I"s, a more comprehensive and impartial view may be obtained, not by patchwork compromises, but through a superhuman effort of transcendence.

The third person singular is distancing and dismissive, says Roland Barthes. "Paul has gone to Peru to do research." Fine. But "*He* has gone to Peru . . . ?" It amounts to a very subtle form of betrayal. "We," by contrast, is a friendly, inclusive word. When I say "we," as I often do, I betray the "I," but that's understandable: self-assertion, however satisfying, must take second place to security in group membership.

"Out of sight, out of mind." Yet it is precisely when my child is out of sight (on his first trip abroad by himself) that he is insistently on my mind. And haven't you had the curious experience that in the midst of a wonderful conversation with a friend, you suddenly wish he would leave so that you can fully savor him? There he is in front of you, talking. But that very fact constitutes a barrier. No animal other than the human is confronted by this paradox.

As a child I was devoted to comics. One of my favorites was a strip called "Ginger," Ginger being the name of a red-haired, all-

American boy who constantly got into trouble. When he was punished by his father, he was apt to cry out indignantly, "How can you do this to me—your own flesh and blood!"

An important difference between modern and traditional society is that the former puts less emphasis on kinship bonds. However, the cry of blood is not so easily stilled. That great figure of the Enlightenment, François Marie Arouet de Voltaire (1694–1778), wrote many plays, all pretty awful because he could not wean himself from the habit of using the device of *voix du sang* (instinctive attraction to kinsfolk) for his scenes of recognition.

Neighborliness, like *community*, is a good word, designating a way of life that is disappearing, to the regret of many. In the old days, people say with a sad shake of the head, neighbors "watched out" for one another. But I say, "Watch out for 'watch out!'" It is ambivalent, and it can mean both caring and idle curiosity. Houses have eyes. Built close, windows gaze into one another. Noises, too, interpenetrate. When houses are built well apart, privacy is better preserved—but not guaranteed. On Shetland Isle, off the coast of Scotland, cottages are at some distance from one another. Yet visual intrusion persists. According to the sociologist Erving Goffman, cottagers of seafaring background use pocket telescopes to keep an eye on their neighbors.

The postmodernist is fond of the word *reflexivity* and is proud to be reflective, even if too much of it can lead to a feeling of airlessness and isolation. But is this new? Giovanni Battista Vico (1668–1744) already noted the tendency in his century. He is well known for challenging the Enlightenment's idea of progress by saying that each age has its own virtues and defects. Only in the heroic age, which combined courage with cruelty and arrogance, could Homer have produced the *Iliad*. Vico's time couldn't have, because it lacked both the requisite social condition and the feverish language. Vico, however, was not sentimental about the distant past, which he described as one of "barbarism of sense." His own time was far more refined, but it suffered from a tendency toward excessive reflection ("barbarism of reflection") that could have the effect of locking individuals into their own barely communicable, private worlds. Doesn't that have a post-modernist ring?

Language isolates. The more an individual knows and the more subtly he is able to say what he knows, the fewer listeners he will have and the more isolated he will feel, even in an academic set-ting. Architectural metaphors help to make clear how this can come about. Graduate students live in sparsely furnished rooms but share a house—the intellectual house of Marx, Gramsci, Foucault, or whoever the favorite thinker happens to be. A won-derful sense of community prevails as the students encounter one another in the hallways and speak a common language, with passwords such as *capital formation, hegemony,* and *the theater of power* to establish firmly their corporate membership. Time passes. As the students mature intellectually, they move from the shared life of a house to rented apartments scattered in the neighborhood. The apartments are close enough that friends still feel free to drop in for visits, and when they do the entire living space comes to life, recapturing as in younger days not only the bonhomie but also the eagerness to embrace wholeheartedly the latest doc-trine. Eventually the students become professors themselves. They begin to build their own houses of intellect and add to the structures as they prosper. Because each house bears witness to a scholar's achievement, it can be a source of considerable personal satisfaction. But the downside is, who will want to visit? And if a colleague does, why should he or she spend time in more than one room?

The Reverend Andrei Davydov is the priest of an Orthodox church located in Pskov, Russia, that dates back to the twelfth century. His calling is the priesthood—and art. "If I were not given a chance to paint, I would probably die," he said in an interview (*New York Times,* March 18, 2000). But he was given a chance, for the walls of the church, used as a garage for the KGB during the Soviet period, were stripped bare. He could use them as his canvas, which he proceeded to do, covering them with religious icons. "What strikes me about icons," Davydov says, "is this ability to create an image of someone you're conversing with. I think all our lives are a search for interlocutors. You decide after years of searching that you can't talk to this person, or that person cannot talk to you. And after more years, you finally decide that the only one you can have a real conversation with is your God."

Suppose someone close to you dies—or so you believe. You mourn, you find life empty, and, eventually, you adjust to this absence by making new friends and setting up new routines. A few years later, you suddenly learn that your friend is alive and wants to reenter your life. Now, be honest. Does your heart leap with joy, or is there just a hint of reservation?

The psychology noted here explains why ghosts are unwelcome. Ghosts are almost always of people we know, people we claim to have loved, people we have mourned. Yet, while they were alive, there were bound to be moments when we wished them out of our hair—dead! One day, to our horror, they unkindly oblige. The guilt we feel is turned into fearsome, accusatory ghosts.

In the *Iliad,* the poet looks down on warriors who have been killed and notes that soon they will be dearer to vultures than to their mothers. Mothers, however, may not know this. The horror of W. W. Jacobs's classic tale "The Monkey's Paw" derives from the reader's chilling awareness that human love—even mother's love—has its limits. The story depicts an old couple who possessed a shriveled monkey's paw that had the power to grant three wishes. Being poor, they wished first for money. A stranger

soon came to deliver it but informed them that the money was
his company's token of sympathy for an accident in which their
son, caught in the wheels of a machine, was killed. The man and
woman buried their son in a nearby cemetery. A few days later,
in the middle of a stormy night, the woman suddenly remembered that the monkey's paw could still grant two more wishes.
She picked it up and asked that her son be returned to her.
Soon—in the time that it would take to walk from the cemetery—there was a loud knock at the door. The woman rushed
downstairs to open it. Her husband tried to stop her, but she
cried, "It's our son, Herbert! Are you afraid of your own son?"
Well, I won't spoil the story. You should be able to guess what
happened next.

The following story, which I heard in the television drama
Ballykissangel, drives home the point of "not belonging" very
well. We have all felt the chill of isolation sometime in our life,
though some no doubt have felt it more often and more intensely
than others. For an unfortunate few, it is almost a permanent
state.

A polar bear cub asks its mother, "Mother, am I a polar bear?"
Mother replies, "Why, of course you are. You have white fur, you
have paws, don't you?" The cub is not satisfied. He goes to his
father and asks, "Dad, am I a polar bear?" Father replies, "Why
do you ask, son? Of course you are. You eat fish, don't you? You
play with the other cubs." The young polar bear then says,
"Why, then, am I so cold?"

Ancestors

In the early 1970s Americans began to shift away from futur-
ism—the idea that they are to be defined by what they can do
in the future—in favor of roots and genealogy, the idea that it
is the past that gives them legitimacy, identity, and pride. To follow the new fashion, I hung my ancestor's portrait in my Minneapolis office. No, it is not Confucius. It is *Homo erectus pekinensis*.

One-upmanship requires that I trace my genealogy as far back as possible.

The Chinese, unlike the ancient Greeks and Mesopotamians, quite early on sought to suppress what they considered to be the less reputable beliefs and practices of their past. Fertility cults, heavy with sex, were made to give way to ancestor cults, which in time became a proud and highly respectable element of Chinese culture. But roots in sex and fertility, however hidden, remained, to be detected by the searching eye. Swedish sinologist Bernard Karlgren convincingly shows that ancestor worship was phallus worship, the ancestral tablet being the representation of an erect phallus. (The right radical of the Chinese word for ancestor—*tzu*—was once an indisputable picture of the male organ. Even in its present form 且 it is rudely suggestive.)

We sometimes envy nonliterate folks for their living tradition. If a tradition is really living, it is a part of the present; it means that ancestors are still looking over our shoulder. Contrary to popular belief, modern society is no different: it, too, is full of living traditions. How can it be otherwise? Not only Einstein but also Newton still haunt our scientific worldview. Modern society differs from folk society in that it has, *in addition to* living tradition, a past that no longer weaves its spell because it is deliberately disengaged from the present and turned into texts that can be criticized, used or not used, as the moderns see fit. In other words, the past for them is no longer fate but choice.

When a proud student-father brings his newborn to me to admire, I say to him, "Well, you are on your way to being an ancestor—a founder of nations." He looks pleasantly surprised that out of his loins (to use a sexy biblical expression) a whole new people can emerge to populate an unimaginably distant future.

We moderns seldom offer respect to our ancestors or even acknowledge their existence. The usual reason given is that we lack piety, that we are too selfishly absorbed in present and future projects to bother with the past. This may be so, but I believe that another reason, more flattering to ourselves, may also be at work. If we moderns do not acknowledge our ancestors and culture heroes, it is because it would take too long. Our ancestors and heroes have given us so many good things (from flush toilets to bypass surgery, from sonnets to human rights) that, even if we want to, we can barely hint at the degree of our indebtedness. By comparison, members of preliterate or folk communities are less burdened. They can show gratitude to their predecessors for passing on to them certain key agricultural skills, social customs, and religious rites, and still have time left over for the practical chores of living.

An ancestor common to all modern humans is named Eve. She is an African, more specifically, a Khoisan. (The Khoisan live in south Africa and are the oldest indigenous people in that part of the continent.) *Science* magazine, which in October 1999 reported this latest pinpointing of Eve based on DNA research, illustrates what our great, great, great, great ... grandmother of 120,000 years ago might have looked like by showing the photo of a modern Khoisan bushwoman from Botswana. Perhaps the United Nations headquarters in New York should put her picture on its walls? How can racism be sustained when we can *see* Eve? Or will this African Eve be too unlike the Eve of glamorizing Western art to be acceptable?

"Latest estimates tell us that of all 'classical' music performed publicly, recorded and broadcast in the West, nearly ninety per cent predates 1900," writes George Steiner in *Real Presences* (1990). How is this for tradition and ancestor worship in the West?

For making a cult of ancestors, Americans are hard to beat. American educators and politicians are constantly invoking the spirit of Washington, Jefferson, Lincoln, and even twentieth-century presidents such as Woodrow Wilson and Franklin Roosevelt. Can you imagine English educators and politicians invoking the spirit of Gladstone, Pitt, or, for that matter, Winston Churchill? The English relegate their ancestors to the past. Americans, in striking contrast, treat theirs as model contemporaries.

Thanksgiving, Christmas. These holiday seasons of familial cheer are times when I am forcefully reminded of the wisdom of Americans, Chinese, and so many other peoples, a wisdom that says: "What really counts in life is your ability to transmit your genes—unless you are Beethoven and can justify your existence by offering the world nine immortal symphonies." Is this view too extreme? Alfred North Whitehead seems to endorse it in a letter to his son dated December 10, 1924.

Sex

The joy of sex is a great gift of nature to the human species. I say the human species, because other sexual animals do not seem capable of enjoying it to anything like the same degree. I watch dolphins copulating, but they can't even embrace—their sexual act seems so passionless. Our closest cousins, the chimpanzees, can embrace, but apparently don't. More often than not, the male merely leans toward the female's back, placing one hand on it, as he makes his insertion. Squeaks of excitement there may be during the intercourse, but no divine madness. So Jane Goodall tells us in *The Chimpanzees of Gombe*. Much of human sexual pleasure derives from touch, not only as two bodies writhe in sweaty entanglement, but also more coolly, though no less pleasurably, as hands run over bare skin.

Why are humans, alone among animals, given this extra incentive to couple? Could it be that, without it, humans with their lively minds would be too distracted by the wonders of the world to do their reproductive duty?

Sex is the longing "to escape my self, to take a holiday in someone else's body" writes Michael Ignatieff in *Scar Tissue*. So here is another plausible answer to the question I raised. Only humans have the sort of self from which they wish to escape; only they feel the need to take a periodic swooning holiday in the body of another.

Human sexuality is undoubtedly enhanced by language. Consider Harry's uncircumcised hard-on in *Rabbit Is Rich*. Nothing special. But John Updike makes it special—makes it into an American poem: "You can feel the foreskin sweetly tug back, like freezing cream lifting the paper cap on the old-time milk bottles."

There is greater intimacy in telling each other experiences of pleasure than experiences of sorrow or pain. The latter is all too common. Much social chitchat is, after all, little else than re-counting mishaps—buses missed, flights canceled, inopportune toothache, the rough time one had with the dentist or the boss. Pleasure is less often admitted for fear of arousing envy. When, then, does a person feel free to confess pleasure, both past and present? One occasion may be the aftermath of sexual congress. The intimacy and mutual delight already achieved can carry over into postcoital conversation. Which is another reason for having sex—good sex.

Love gives one the right to look at the beloved—to see the shape of the moon over each fingernail. "I tell you this: you'll never know the body like I know it. The lines beneath his eyes.

Do you know how many there are, do you know that one has less than the other? And the scar behind his ear, and the hairs in his nostrils, which has the most, what colour they are in what light?" Thus a homosexual man taunts his female rival in John Osborne's play *A Patriot for Me*. Dwelling lovingly on the details of the beloved's body seems to me more characteristic of women than of men. Biology has given women a head start in exploring attentively every nook and corner, crease and bulge, of their baby.

A good account of erotic play between very young children is provided by the Greek author Nikos Kazantzakis, drawing on his own experience, in *Report to Greco*. He was three years old and his female playmate four. One day, she took his hand and brought him into her mother's house. "Without losing a moment, we took off our socks, lay down on our backs, and glued our bare soles together. We did not breathe a word. Closing my eyes, I felt Emine's warmth pass from her soles to mine, then ascend little by little to my knees, belly, breast, and fill me entirely. The delight I experienced was so profound that I thought I would faint."

Jan Myrdal, son of Gunnar and Alva Myrdal, was a precocious child, highly imaginative in every way, including the sexual. As an eleven-year-old, he reports in his autobiography, he liked to take out his copy of *Alice in Wonderland* to look furtively at the picture of Alice falling down the rabbit hole. What's wrong with that? Nothing, except that in the boy's guileful eyes Alice had her arms raised over her head and her skirt blown up to reveal her navel. The boy wanted "to see her naked. Her cunt, too." In the boy's imagination, Alice was smiling rather than alarmed. Her smile made her his accomplice.

Should parents ban *Alice*?

Pier Paolo Pasolini is said to have had sex with two boys
every night, after which he would return home all energized to
write. In the course of a lifetime, he wrote some twenty thousand
pages of noteworthy prose and poetry. André Gide could have as
many as seven orgasms a day, again with boys as stimuli. Gide
wrote less, but he did win the Nobel Prize. Makes one queasy,
doesn't it, to know that boys' bodies were used to fuel literary
production?

Gay man gives elegant parties, with sparkling dinnerware,
fresh linen, choice food and wine, in a tastefully furnished apartment. Guests arrive on time, as does everything else from hors
d'oeuvre to liqueur. When a gay man enters the heterosexual
world, he is immediately struck by its general air of chaos: nothing is quite in place or on time, and the reason, of course, is children. Once a child is born, it is as though weather in all its
moods has entered the heart of the household, infusing into it
springlike freshness some of the time and the violence of a tornado other times.

Gay sex is "objectively disordered," according to the Roman
Catholic Church. "Objective disorder" behind closed doors
leaves plenty of time and energy for the ordered world of culture. Heterosexuality is "objectively ordered," yet its effect
(children) is to introduce a state of haphazardness that makes
civilized living, without nannies and servants, almost impossible.

Yves Saint Laurent is one of the most admired couturiers of
our time. In February 1992, he celebrated the thirtieth anniver-
sary of his couture house with a party at the Opéra Bastille, attended by "tout Paris." What a successful career and, at the same
time, what a sad life of loneliness, clinical depression, alco-
holism, and addiction to cocaine. Saint Laurent is devoted to the
woman's body. He spent his entire adult life draping it so that
women might envy and men might be enthralled. Bitter irony,

isn't it? For, as a homosexual, surely his fondest wish is that men be drawn to *him*, not to his rivals. And yet here he is, adorning them with passion!

Haute couture has more than its share of homosexuals. Strange that this should be the case. I would have thought that heterosexual men would dominate the profession, for what could be better for them than to hover around, touch, and measure beautiful women every day? Or do I see here support for the (extreme) feminist view that men are more inclined to do violence than adore, or make love to, women?

In my book *The Good Life*, I describe various kinds of interpersonal experience important, if not critical, to the good life. Among them is sexual conjugation. How does one get this experience across in words? Some writers try earthy detail and specificity, others (Iris Murdoch, for example) evocative generality. What is sexual love like? "Suddenly the reorientation of the world round one illumined point, all else in shadow. The total alteration of corporeal being, the minute electric sensibility of the nerves, the tender expectancy of the skin. The omnipresence of a ghostly sense of touch. The awareness of organs. The absolute demand for the presence of the beloved, the categorical imperative, the beauty of all things."

Readers naturally assume that the act is between a man and a woman. Actually, in *The Philosopher's Pupil*, it is between two guys. I slipped in this passage out of all the heterosexual ones I could have chosen. I have not been straight with my readers.

Can someone who has no ear for the Christian story really appreciate Dante's *Divine Comedy*, Bach's *St. Matthew Passion*, or Eliot's *Four Quartets*? Subtle thinkers have argued back and forth. I bring it up only to open a different, though related, question. Can a homosexual really appreciate literature the center stage of which is sexual love between a man and a woman? For myself, I have to say yes and no. The yes comes out of the fact that in much of literature before the twentieth century writers use words to evoke the erotic rather than the sexual. An outstanding example is Shakespeare's *Romeo and Juliet*. If there is sexual charge in the play, it exudes from the sexiness of the young players, as in Zeffirelli's movie version, and not from Shakespeare's poetry, which is far too elevated to capture the heat and odor of the groin. As for the no, well, in all nude scenes, including the one in Zeffirelli's movie, my appreciation of them has to be distanced: too close, and I feel slightly queasy, as surely heterosexuals do when they witness homosexual couplings.

In the bad days before the sexual revolution, gay boys had considerable difficulty satisfying their need for erotic stimulation, in contrast to heterosexual boys, who enjoyed a surfeit not so much from pornographic magazines, which were difficult for them to obtain before 1950, but from mainline advertisements of everything from perfume to automobiles, all of which used images of nubile young women to pitch their sale. So what could gay boys do and not have their sexual orientation exposed? Answer: they could read *National Geographic,* and they could do so right in front of their censorious parents. Before (say) 1960, that magazine frequently showed handsome, half-naked young males of the Third World: Indonesian hunter-gatherers, Polynesian fishermen and divers, Sudanese herdsmen and athletes.

Recent issues of *National Geographic* still feature young males from the Third World, but they are clothed in Wal-Mart shirts and shorts. And thank God they are, for their bodies are now about as sexually arousing as those of overweight Wisconsinites. Economic development is to blame. Having given up heavy outdoor work in favor of office jobs, the young men of other lands have lost not only their culture but also their good looks. Meanwhile, gay boys in affluent societies, liberated from the closet and catered to by an ever indulgent consumer society, can satisfy their sexual fantasies with over-the-counter magazines.

A great experience in nature's gift is sex. Another is "to start the morning with a satisfactory dump" (W. H. Auden). A pity that good poetry can't be written to honor the dump. With poetry's help, the dump—along with food, which is part of the same alimentary process—can take over some of sex's role in providing us with our daily requirement of respectable, yet intense, sensual satisfaction.

Male and Female

The human male, it would seem, is a water-added version of the human female. A woman's body is 55 to 65 percent water, whereas a man's body is 65 to 75 percent water. One consolation for the male is that, by virtue of the greater water content of his body, he can hold more liquor.

In America, men have a more romantic attitude toward their partner than women. Men, rather than women, are more likely to say, "We are perfect for each other." In a survey of college students, 65 percent of the men, but only 24 percent of the women say they will not marry someone that they are not in love with, even if the person has all the other qualities they desire. "Perhaps men are more romantic because they are less responsible for 'working on' the emotional aspects of the relationship, and therefore see love as magically and perfectly present or absent," writes Francesca M. Cancian in *Love in America*.

A woman looks at the newborn infant and sees nature in the raw. Even to her fond maternal eyes, it surely can't be judged very intelligent or a great beauty. She knows, however, that with attentive care the infant will turn into an adorable baby, and then into an intelligent and chatty toddler. A man seldom participates fully in these early stages. By the time he is more involved, the children are old enough to seem to have certain fixed characteristics and capabilities: this one is a good athlete, that one a good mathematician or poet, and so on. A man is therefore likely to think that hard work and training can help a talent grow, but only up to a point. A woman, by contrast, has far greater faith in hard work and training. For her, even the seemingly ungifted (remember that stupid, bawling infant!) can, given the right encouragement and circumstance, become accomplished. She is naturally more sympathetic, a greater believer in the possibilities of effort, than romantic man.

Political empowerment may be the end of leisure and the death of creativity. Talented women should think twice before accepting positions of political or administrative power. Their time and energy may be totally absorbed in using it. Don't be fooled by the men. They may cunningly cede power to "mom," thus forcing her to take care of the budget and other tedious household chores, leaving them the leisure to draw on the living-room wall, make stink bombs, and otherwise creatively play.

"Look, son, when I was your age . . ." But he is not my son. It is American usage for an older man to call a younger man "son." Yet no middle-aged woman would call a younger woman, who is a mere acquaintance or stranger, "daughter." Why not? One answer may lie in the sort of power play so habitual among men: applying the label "son" to a young male—a potential rival—diminishes him. But I believe another factor is at work: male promiscuity and the male's inability to keep track of the wild oats he has sown. A man is aware that, implausible as it may be, the good-looking youngster bagging his groceries is his own flesh and blood. Women also engage in power play among themselves, but they would not risk putting down a rival by calling her "daughter," for "daughter" connotes youth, a highly valued attribute in woman. Women also do not use the word indiscriminately because they know who their daughters are—unless an infant is stolen at birth, hardly a common event. What does all this say about the nature and intensity of male, as distinct from female, bonding across the generations?

"Oh boy" is an expression that I've heard some women use. It is a lovely exclamation of joy. But does anyone (male or female) ever say "Oh girl"? If not, why not?

~·

"That's the worst of girls," said Edmund to Peter and the Dwarf [in *Prince Caspian*, by C. S. Lewis]. "They never carry a map in their heads."

"That's because our heads have something inside them," said Lucy.

Touché!

~·

The gender bias in Western civilization impressed itself force-fully on me when I heard Handel's *Messiah* during the Christmas holidays. "For unto us a Child is born." The child, it turns out, is a boy. Won't girls feel marginalized as choirs and congrega-tions belt out that gendered word? Perhaps the gender of the child could be changed in alternate performances: boy one sea-son, girl the next.

> For unto us a Child is born, unto us a Daughter is
> given,
> and the government shall be upon Her shoulder, and
> Her name
> shall be called Wonderful, Counsellor, the Mighty
> Goddess, the
> Everlasting Mother, the Princess of Peace.

Has anything theologically important been introduced thereby? Surely not, since the Child is a Divine Being who tran-scends gender. And yet . . .

~·

A Presbyterian minister, called on to preach on short notice at a service Queen Victoria was to attend, was understandably nervous. He offered a prayer that was intended to be eloquent, as suited the glorious occasion, but came out as: "Grant that as she

grows to be an old woman she may be made a new man; and
that in all righteous causes she may go forth before her people a
he-goat on the mountains." (*Anglican Digest*, vol. 33, no. 6, 1991)

Eugenia Zukerman, quoted in the *New York Times* (February 22,
1981), says that we often hear people say "She played like a man"
but rarely (if ever) "He played like a woman," even though the
terms used to commend the qualities of musical interpretations
may be feminine—*grace, elegance,* and *charm,* for example. Zukerman goes on to suggest that there may be a subconscious sexual
reason for male instrumental supremacy: a man with an external
"instrument" seems perfectly natural, whereas a woman performing with such an instrument can seem unnatural.

In a letter to Ann Landers, a proud mother reports that her
fifteen-year-old son plays football and takes guitar lessons; his
fourteen-year-old sister is a cheerleader and takes voice lessons.
The boy offers his instrument, the girl offers herself. These
stereotypes are changing, though years may have to pass before
their reversal causes no surprise. Meanwhile, it is most unlikely
that a mother will boast that her son is a cheerleader and takes
voice lessons and his sister plays football and takes guitar lessons.

Hugh MacDiarmid, in a poem, notes that while he loves his
little son, he could not confine himself to the child's bedside
when he was ill. He grew impatient of the child's "squalid little
needs" and longed for the large, bustling world outside. Yet
the child's mother had no trouble attending to "the dread level"
of nothing but life itself and stayed with the child until he
recovered.

One of the successes of the women's liberation movement is
to make more men attend to life's "squalid little needs."

In books published before 1960, you can count on finding
something like this in the acknowledgments: "And last but not

least, I thank my wife, without whose typing skills and encouragement this book never could have seen the light of day." Now I
ask, was this true or sincere? It might have been sincere, but surely
not true, for books continue to be written and published without
a devoted wife at one's side. But maybe they are not as good?

Can a woman imagine what it is like to be a man, and vice
versa? Perhaps. But we need evidence. Marguerite Yourcenar, in
her historical novel *Memoirs of Hadrian,* attempts to get inside the
feelings and thoughts of a Roman emperor. Has she been wholly
successful? Would a male reader find her portrait entirely convincing? Male writers have apparently succeeded in creating immortal female characters: Madame Bovary and Anna Karenina
jump to mind. The critical question, however, is not just the
rightness of the external observations but the rightness of the
emotion felt from the inside. Surely only a woman can know
that, and only she has any real hope of portraying it convincingly. Yet when Nadine Gordimer was asked, on the occasion of
her receiving the Nobel Prize for Literature, how she felt about
portraying a black or male character from the inside, she responded, "What about James Joyce's Molly Bloom soliloquy in
Ulysses? Here's a man who described the most intimate feelings of
a woman; in my opinion, none of us, none of the women, have
ever approached this." (*Time,* October 14, 1991)

Culturally, a large majority of people in all times and places
have celebrated heterosexual love and union. Millennial accu-
mulations in works of art, music, and literature, and (in modern
times) movie and television drama have only one basic message:
the naturalness, the goodness, and the beauty of a Romeo
embracing a Juliet. How can a male who loves another male
read the following heterosexual paean by John Updike (in
Self-Consciousness) without a sense of exclusion, a tinge of sadness,
a wish to protest while knowing that to protest is somehow always to protest too much?

Watching the Olympic Games ice-dancing the other night
on television, I was struck by the primordial poetry of a
man and woman together—each sex with its different
fleshly center of emphasis and style of contour, each with
its special biological assignment and evolved social expectations, but partnered, mutually compensatory, supportive
and amusing and excitingly, maddeningly strange to each
other, together making a single species. As the couples
flashed and glided over the ice, intertwining, some sweet
brute truth hulked dimly out of animal past, from near
where sex was invented by the algae and ferns, and I
wanted to cry in joy, feeling humanity mine and the ice-
dancers', as a spot of warmth within vast dark coldness.

The Chinese writer Lin Yutang (famous in the 1930s and
1940s) said that after a few hours of intensive work he felt as
fragile and pale as a leaf pressed between the pages of a book.
He would descend from his upstairs study into the dining room,
fragrant with the odor of food, and into the round arms of his
earth-mother wife, who considered it her job to restore to him
his chlorophyll—his green fuse of life. Sexist, of course. We
shudder at such male presumption. Nowadays, men and women
work at equally demanding jobs. They return home equally wan
and exhausted. Neither is able to offer the other chicken soup.
What has to give? The quality of the work?

Chinese society is patriarchal, yet not macho. Consider *The
Story of the Stone,* a much read and esteemed novel written by Cao
Xueqin in the middle of the eighteenth century. The author
himself, looking back to his youth, remembered the girls he had
known as all "morally and intellectually [his] superior." He passed
this view on to the novel's boy hero, Bao Yu, who was made to
say that "the pure essence of humanity was all concentrated in
the female of the species and . . . males were its mere dregs and
off-scourings." Elsewhere, Bao Yu was made to say that "girls are

made of water and boys are made of mud," and that only when he was with girls did he feel "fresh and clean."

Taoism considers water (feminine) to be superior to rock (masculine). Confucianism seems to favor the yang (masculine) principle, yet its governmental ideal is *wu wei,* which means "no action," and the power of the emperor himself is best exhibited by sitting perfectly still. No privileging of male initiative and restlessness there! In Chinese society, the expression "pale-faced scholar" is a compliment rather than a nasty dig at one's manhood, as it could be in the West. Although China was an empire through much of its history, its warriors enjoyed high regard only if they were clever strategists and wrote competent poetry.

Power

What do we want out of life? Love, admiration, respect, honor, prestige, money, and so on. Maybe it all amounts to power. Even love, for as Henry Kissinger says, power is a great aphrodisiac. We academics are not free to be too open about what we want. Mobsters feel no such compunction. So, let's hear what a mobster has to say. To a reporter's question, "Why be a mobster? What's so great about it?" he replied: "It's the greatest thing a human could experience.... When you sneeze, 15 handkerchiefs come out. I mean, everywhere you go, people just can't do enough for you. At Christmas people are hangin' on your door, dropping off gifts. If it rains, 25 umbrellas open up. If you walk into a restaurant, they'll chase the person out of the best table and put you there. There is just so much glamor and respect and money.... In the Mob, you've got friends, you belong to an army, something that is powerful. You're with the elite. Your word is law." (*Time,* June 17, 1991)

Power is command over time rather than space. A powerful man may choose to occupy a small office and live in a modest house, but he will not yield time—the one possession he does not have more of than anyone else. Who is more powerful? Well, who waits for whom? Louis XIV, it is said, never had to wait for anyone. On one occasion, the Sun King stepped into the audience hall barely a second or two after the courtier he had summoned entered. The King was aghast. "J'ai failli attendre!" ("I just missed having to wait!")

The lover is one who waits. Hence, says Roland Barthes, there is always something pathetic about him.

In a short story by Primo Levi (in *The Mirror Maker*), a man called M walked down a dark narrow street and saw a husky lad in a T-shirt coming toward him. M felt uneasy, for there was no way to avoid collision unless he laid flat against the wall to let the other pass. Would the youth, a sailor who looked menacing, demand money? No. After a while, it became clear that he wanted M to lie on the ground. Which M did. The sailor bent over and patiently pressed down M's bent knee so that he was stretched out flat on his back. He then walked over him, placing his foot first on one part, then on another part, of the body. And that was it—all done in silence. M got up and dusted himself off. He was unhurt, but he could not for the rest of the day—or ever after—fully recover his sense of self-worth.

Levi was incarcerated in Auschwitz. He probably remembered that one of the things the guards did to inmates was to force them to lie on the ground and become a human carpet, which the guards trampled over back and forth. Levi died in 1987, an apparent suicide.

Power is prestige, the root meaning of which is magic or sleight of hand. There was an outpouring of grief in the nation when John F. Kennedy Jr. died in an airplane crash at age thirty-eight. People lined up outside his New York residence to pay homage. A twenty-nine-year-old salesman, Anthony Owens, was among them and in tears. Several years ago, Owens made a delivery to Kennedy's office building and spied him in the corridor. "I froze," he said. "Then I started shaking like this." He extended a trembling hand. "Mr. Kennedy asked me why I was so nervous and I said, 'You're a part of American history.' He told me that he was just like anybody else and offered me an autograph if I held the elevator" (*New York Times*, July 22, 1999).

Isn't this remarkable? We have long passed the age of sacred kings, and yet, at the end of the second millennium, in a high-tech democratic nation, one young citizen trembled in awe at the sight of another. And pundits say that we modern people live in a disenchanted world. If only it were so.

The sinologist Simon Leys tells a story, dating back to the T'ang dynasty (608–917), that illustrates the soul-blighting effects of Oriental despotism—effects that continue to mar Chinese mentality and manners in modern times: "The younger brother of an official prepares to leave for his first posting. He promises his elder brother that he will be . . . patiently obedient in all his dealings with his superior. 'If they spit on me, I shall simply wipe my face without a word.' 'Oh, no!' replies the elder brother, aghast. 'They might take your gesture for an impudence. Let the spittle dry by itself.'"

Sadistic power aims at reducing another human being to an animal or a machine, obedient to the master or owner's every wish. In some plantation homes of the antebellum South, slave boys, fully mature physically, had to wait on table wearing a shirt that was barely long enough to cover their private parts (Winthrop D. Jordan, *White over Black*, 1968). As for reducing humans to mechanical toys, the anarchist-geographer Peter Kropotkin had this to say in *Memoirs of a Revolutionist:* In the reign of Nicholas I, an admired military man was a person "whose soldiers were trained to perform almost superhuman tricks with their legs and rifles; and who could show on parade a row of soldiers as perfectly aligned and as motionless as a row of toy-soldiers. 'Very good,' the Grand Duke Mikhael said once of a

regiment, after having kept it for one hour presenting arms—
'only, they *breathe!*'"

Professional athletes in the United States earn fabulous
salaries and are lionized in schools and Rotary Clubs. On the
other hand, they can be "owned" and "sold." On October 14,
1981, the New York Yankees defeated Oakland 13 to 3. An
Associated Press photo shows the proud and grinning owner of
the Yankees, George Steinbrenner, patting the cheek of ball-
player Oscar Gamble, who is black. Patting the cheek! Gamble
was bare-chested; Steinbrenner had on a coat, and his out-
stretched arm exposed the tip of his shirt sleeve and handsome
cufflinks.

I suspect that I can enjoy exploiting others, but only if it can
be done in the old-fashioned, personal way. The closest I got to
this pleasure was when my kitchen sink needed the service of a
plumber. A young guy arrived, stretched out on his back on the
floor, and went to work with a heavy wrench. He writhed this
way and that, his legs thrashed about, and soon sweat trickled
down his forehead and neck. And I? I leaned over the kitchen
counter to watch, nursing in my hands a freshly brewed cup of
cappuccino. His revenge—this being modern capitalist society—was to send me a monstrous bill!

Power, as I have said, can seek to reduce a human being to an
animal or a mechanical toy. There is a third way, unique to our
age: the power to demand truth. Judges investigating crime have
always had this right. In modern fascist and communist states,
however, authorities exercise it over their citizens under any and
all circumstances. No one is allowed to withhold information.
The humiliation is all the greater, says Milan Kundera in *Immortality*, in that the information demanded is often of a purely factual

nature. Having to answer large (philosophical) questions such as "Do you believe in God?" or "Do you recognize the state's ultimate authority over moral issues?" may be intrusive or even have fatal consequence, but it can be done with a certain dignity. This is not the case when citizens are forced to tell truthfully, "Where did you have dinner on the night of September 23?" and "Have you ever had sex with A and, if so, when and where?" Not having the right to keep facts to oneself reduces one to infantilism.

We disapprove of imperialism—political, economic, and even cultural. But what about intellectual imperialism, the power of an idea to convince? To con*vince*, as the root meaning of that word suggests, is to vanquish—to render an opponent defenseless and naked by the sheer force of one's argument. Bertrand Russell was once so vanquished by D. H. Lawrence. Poor Russell. For a time he contemplated suicide. But he came to his senses and covered his nakedness with what some would say was armor.

The novelist Flannery O'Connor wrote in a letter: "You have to be able to dominate the existence that you characterize. That is why I write about people who are more or less primitive. I couldn't dominate a Miss [Simone] Weil because she is more intelligent and better than I am" (*Letters of Flannery O'Connor*). No wonder even the greatest writers have not been able to create a convincing saint. A writer is a sort of tyrant, but no tyrant has real power over a saint.

Blarney, according to Andrew Greeley and William McCready, is "the capacity never to mean what one says and never to say what one means. Anyone who has attempted to get a *straight* answer when wandering through the west of Ireland must be alive to this possibility."

More generally, rambling incoherent speech is characteristic of the powerless. People accustomed to power are forceful and direct. Think of the drill sergeant, the schoolteacher, and the English aristocrat. In academia, compare the direct and concise prose of physicists with the windiness of social scientists and the blarney of new humanists. Guess who are paid the most and who the least.

~

No one can maintain his or her dignity in a hospital. André Malraux, minister of culture in the DeGaulle government and a grand mandarin of modern art, was hospitalized at age seventy for a serious nervous disorder. One day he tried to walk. A young nurse caught him and said, "Oh, you young rascal!"

~

"Knowledge is power"—a saying that goes back to antiquity. But it received a boost in the eighteenth century when long voyages across the oceans were increasingly common. Also increasingly common was the threat of mutiny by harshly treated and disgruntled sailors. Mutiny was kept in check, however, by the captain's knowledge. Only he and his chief officers knew the arts of celestial navigation. Throw the navigators overboard—throw knowledge overboard—and the sailors courted death.

And now, in a fit of fantasy, I see the mutiny as nevertheless occurring because the sailors were protopostmodernists. To them, the captain's dance around the sextant (invented in 1731) was just that, rather than a powerful technique for determining location. So they tossed the captain overboard and trusted their own dance to bring them safely home.

Education, Teaching, Knowledge

Education is "the training of human souls," according to Alfred North Whitehead.

~

The word *consider* means "seeing the stars together, as constellations, or in relation to one another." What a beautiful word!

No wonder I am always urging students to "consider this," or "consider that." I have to confess, though, that until recently I did not know that I was asking them to make constellations out of stars.

The late medieval university maintained a core curriculum of "soft" subjects for beginning students. These included natural philosophy, mathematics, and logic. Good students went beyond them to the "tough" subjects of law, medicine, and theology. And so they moved from the simple to the complex, from atoms and space to social institutions and, ultimately, God. In our time, students also move from the less to the more difficult, only the subjects have been reversed. Now the dull take up the challenge of understanding complex human phenomena and social institutions, whereas the bright devote themselves to understanding the relatively simple laws of physical reality.

In the sixteenth century, English aristocrats realized that they could no longer count on brawn (their warrior heritage) for power and prestige. Their way of adapting to the future was to send their sons to school, to Harrow and Eton, Oxford and Cambridge, which up to that time were attended primarily by the sons of the struggling class. Aristocrats knew that the subjects taught there—Latin, Greek, theology—were pretty useless for practical affairs. Wisely, they also knew that these subjects did offer one thing—difficulty. Confronting and overcoming intellectual difficulty would prepare the young man's mind and, indeed, his character to live in a world that was changing rapidly. Is there a lesson here for aspiring minorities in the United States?

Obesity used to be a symbol of wealth and social status. Now that even the poor can be obese (at least in the developed countries), it no longer has prestige—indeed, quite the opposite. Ralph Lauren Polo shirts and BMWs used to be symbols of wealth and social status. Now that even young drug traffickers can afford them, they have lost much of their sheen. So what remains? And what will remain in the foreseeable future? Answer: an education that requires the prolonged and rigorous training of the mind. Eggheads, even now, have surprising prestige in the general public. A study sponsored by Madison Avenue shows that a Harvard Nobel laureate in chemistry and a famous writer can sell more hardware than can either a rock star or a professional athlete. ("Sweet Shopping at Sears," *Science*, September 30, 1994)

We take for granted that liberal education—exposure to the world's greatest works of art and literature—is good for us. But what is the evidence? And in what ways "good"? Raymond Carver, the American short-story writer, is among those who are not only disappointed but puzzled: "I remember in my twenties reading plays by Strindberg, a novel by Max Frisch, Rilke's poetry, listening all night to music by Bartók, watching a TV special on the Sistine Chapel and Michelangelo and feeling in each case that my life had to change after these experiences, it couldn't help but be affected by these experiences and changed. There was simply no way I would not become a different person. But then I found out soon enough my life was not going to change after all. Not in any way that I could see, perceptible or otherwise." (*Writers at Work: The Paris Interviews*, 1986)

Nothing is more useful—more practical—than a liberal education, for what it teaches is no less than how to get more out of life, more savor in day-to-day living. For example, thanks to the Roman emperor and Stoic Marcus Aurelius, I now have greater appreciation for a loaf of bread. In the *Meditations*, he notes: "We ought to observe that even the things which follow unexpectedly from the things that are produced according to nature contain something pleasing and attractive. For instance, when bread is baked some parts are split at the surface, and these parts that thus open are open contrary to the purpose of the baker's art, and yet are beautiful in a peculiar manner; and they in a peculiar way excite a desire for eating."

Here are two charming stories about how the English, even among the humble, valued education. The English could hardly have risen to greatness in the early modern age without a respect for learning up and down the layers of society.

One July day in 1667, Samuel Pepys and his friends went for a stroll up the Epsom Downs, where they encountered a shepherd and his little boy. The boy was reading the Bible to his father. "So I made the boy read to me," said Pepys, "which he did with the forced tone that children usually read, that was mighty pretty." Pepys and his friends complimented the father, who, his chest swelling with pride, "blessed God" for his little boy.

The second story occurred a century later. A water boy rowed Dr. Johnson and Boswell down the Thames to Greenwich. The friends were discussing the shaping influence of classical culture. Boswell thought people didn't need it. Johnson reluctantly agreed. "For instance," he said, "this boy rows us well without learning as if he could sing the song of Orpheus to Argonauts, who were the first sailors." Then he interrupted himself and called to the boy: "What would you give, my lad, to know about the Argonauts?" "Sir," said the boy, "I would give what I have."

A dangerous educational myth in America, convenient to adults who (for one reason or another) wish to shirk their responsibility to teach, is that children learn best from their peers. They do. They learn street smarts and power politics—who is strong and must be deferred to, who is weak and can be exploited. They learn, in other words, what young chimpanzees learn. They do *not* learn the feeding habits of dinosaurs, the importance of zero in mathematics, why stars sparkle, and why it is more blessed to give than to receive. They do not learn how to be distinctly—uniquely—human.

On the other hand, how much could one have learned from President Eliot of Harvard? John McCormick relates in *Santayana* that Eliot ran into George Santayana in the yard (in 1900?) and asked him how his philosophy class was doing. Santayana replied that his students were making progress through Plato and should soon move on to Aristotle. "No, no, Santayana, what I meant by my enquiry is, how many students have enrolled for your lectures?"

Young Americans will do anything to get an education, working full time during the summer and part time in the academic year. To help pay for tuition, they sell their labor and they may have to sell their blood. But that's not all. In a college magazine, I read that male students at the University of California at Berkeley are selling their semen! They do so twice or three times a week at sperm banks suitably equipped with stimulating magazines. "I consider it a job," Eric says, "like any other job." A flexible schedule is one of the job's attractions—that and the pay.

Alexandre Grothendieck, one of France's most distinguished mathematicians, turned down his share ($135,000) of the prestigious Crawford Prize of the Royal Swedish Academy of Science (*Science*, May 13, 1988). Grothendieck gave two reasons for his surprising action. One: as a professor at the University of Montpellier he already has enough to live on. Two: only the passage of time can show whether his ideas are truly fertile. His second reason reinforces my belief that the teaching awards that universities now regularly hand out, under society's pressure, are ill-advised. Immediate evaluations by students cannot be very useful if good teaching—really good teaching—is the imparting of ideas and aspirations that prove fertile months, even years, after the event.

It is hard to teach young Americans at a state university because their social backgrounds, hence expectations and behavior, are so different. Take the following two examples. I work in my office with the door open, being more stimulated than distracted by the sound of footsteps in the hallway. One day, a student passing by entered my office, went to my desk, took out a sheaf of Kleenex, blew his nose, threw it into the wastepaper bin, and then walked out—all without saying a single word. At the other extreme—true, this extreme happens more often—my office phone rings, I pick it up, and I announce my name. Silence at the other end. Then comes a hesitant voice that says, "Oh, I thought I would be speaking to your secretary!"

A new grad student asks me, "How would you like to be addressed—Mister, Doctor, Professor, or your given name?" I hear the question with increasing frequency as the age gap yawns. My answer is this: "Oh, call me anything you like. But, if I were you, I would use a more formal form of address—not out of deference, but for selfish reasons. For you see, if you address me by my title, you will be reminding me of my duties to you. And it is to your advantage to do so. On the other hand, if you call me by my first name, you are saying that we are buddies—a relationship that gives me permission to exploit your youth. I shall feel free to ask you for help with such heavy chores as moving the furniture and clearing off the snow. And, of course, given my age and feebleness, you can hardly ask me to do the same for you."

Confucius said: "Only one who bursts with eagerness do I instruct; only one who bubbles with excitement do I enlighten. If I hold up one corner and a man cannot come back to me with the other three, I do not continue the lesson" (*Analects*, book 7, chapter 8). Confucius didn't have to worry about enrollment.

To arrive at the truth (verity) is hard work: it calls for discipline—severity. The French don't need to be reminded because their word for truth is *vérité. Vérité et Séverité* is a slogan of the Fifth Republic.

Customers in a capitalist society are encouraged to be thoroughly *un*disciplined in their buying habits. If we keep telling students that they are our customers—and don't forget, customers are always right—why would any student-customer buy into discipline? That word suggests constraint. And discipline does indeed constrain, as logic or rigor in any endeavor constrains. Its end result, however, is liberation. In contrast, material goods, the acquisition of which supposedly opens up the consumer's world, end by enslaving him.

Charles Darwin's *Autobiography* contains much that should encourage a student who feels that he or she is not very clever, for Darwin himself—one of the world's certified geniuses—wrote: "I have no great quickness of apprehension or wit which is so remarkable in some clever men, for instance, [Thomas] Huxley. I am therefore a poor critic: a paper or book, when I first read it, generally excites my admiration, and it is only after considerable reflection that I perceive weak points."

Darwin doesn't seem aware that he is describing an advantage rather than a handicap. Unlike his quick-witted friends who go into a book with darts all ready to fly and therefore can hardly learn anything from it, Darwin with his receptivity—his readiness to admire—can always pick up some useful facts or even an insight before applying the dismissive intellect. Charity, it turns out, is highly desirable even in operations of the mind.

"Emotional involvement," says Paul Robinson of Stanford University, "is inherent in all teaching, if one takes the job seriously. The process of enlightenment is also a process of seduction—which is another way of saying that teaching is a form of sublimation" (*Salmagundi*, Winter 1983).

No wonder I take harsh criticism from students badly. It is as though my declaration of love has been spurned. Critical comments from colleagues are, by contrast, easier to accept. Bald and wrinkled like myself, they have never been the serious objects of my seduction.

The last time I saw John E. Kesseli, my dissertation adviser of more than forty years ago, was in 1976. He suffered acutely from emphysema at the time. He could barely walk; fits of coughing periodically doubled him over. We both knew that this would be our last meeting. In his office, we carried on a social conversation, reluctant to see it coming to an end. When at last I stood up to leave, I could see my old mentor struggling to say something nice about my work. This was difficult, for after I left Berkeley I became what he had prognosticated and feared—a high-flying "philosophical" geographer. Finally, at the door, he mumbled, "About your recent work, well, if you can get away with it, I guess it's OK." I was touched. Nevertheless, ever since I have lived in dread of being tapped on the shoulder by some gimlet-eyed guardian of academic virtue.

China's first emperor, who died in 210 B.C., ordered the construction of the Great Wall and the destruction of books. Both acts were directed against the threat of chaos. The Great Wall, by keeping out the barbarians, maintained spatial order. Book burning, by eradicating the momentum of past events and the turbulence of radical ideas, maintained temporal order.

Several noted writers have associated talent with a sort of driven energy—a primal force—rather than just a knack for doing something well. Thus Theodor Adorno: "Talent is perhaps

nothing other than successfully sublimated rage." Thus Gerald
Brenan: "In the old Provençal or Limousin language talent (*talens,
talanz, talans*) meant desire, longing, inclination. In Dante's
'Divine Comedy,' talento means lust." And thus Wittgenstein:
"Genius is talent exercised with courage."

The ideal university, then, is a place of courage, rage, and lust!

Strange, isn't it, that both American students and stuffy Victorians believe in being "cool"? For both, it is bad form to seem
too curious or enthusiastic. "Curiosity" is no virtue to Matthew
Arnold and a vice to Nietzsche. As for "enthusiasm," it is dismissed as a bad habit of people with little education who are
easily swayed by fads and outlandish doctrines. Ronald Knox
(1888–1957), a distinguished theologian with more than a bit of
the Victorian in him, wrote a whole book on Christian heresies,
called *Enthusiasm*.

Partitioning of domestic space—a separate room for every conceivable activity—reached a peak in the Victorian period. Knowledge and feeling, too, came to be highly compartmentalized.
Victorians made life easy for themselves by not mixing the categories. Religion was religion, art was art. The Sermon on the
Mount, considered religious admonition in the church, was poetry
in the home. Friendship was friendship, sex was sex, which made
it possible for one man to write love letters to another man without sensing that he had moved dangerously close to the precipice
of homosexuality. Freud's great revolution was to remove some of
the partitions such that not only the murderous kitchen flowed
into the polite dining room and the polite dining room flowed
into the living room of witty discourse, but (so to speak) doors
also have been removed from the doubtfully respectable bathroom
and bedroom. Unlike the Victorians', our psychic and mental
houses have few walls. We are forced to wonder, more or less constantly, how one area of knowledge or feeling relates to another.

Does travel broaden the mind? Consider Immanuel Kant.
He never left Königsberg all his life. He was a profound philosopher, but his work on geography left much to be desired, being
based almost wholly on hearsay and secondary sources. An old
Saturday Review cartoon (in a series called "Through History with
J. Wesley Smith") shows a self-satisfied burgher, just returned
from a business trip abroad, wagging his finger at Kant and saying, "You, Kant, should travel more and broaden your mind."
Travel broadens the mind. That, perhaps, is the trouble.

A scholar who disdains a house that is cluttered with useless
objects may yet clutter his mind with useless knowledge. Seneca
(died A.D. 65) already complained of pedants who "want to
know how many oarsmen Ulysses had, whether the *Iliad* or the
Odyssey was written first . . . and other questions of this kind."
He believed it to be a Greek disease that, in his time, had spread
to the Romans.

In old age, the Cambridge classicist F. L. Lucas regretted the
years he had spent on third-rate literature in order to write and
publish scholarly papers. He wished he had spent more time on
the great books. Had he done so, his scholarly reputation would
have suffered, but the quality of his life would have improved.

Social science can make progress in a technical area (demo-
graphic statistics, for example), as other sciences do. But what it
chooses to examine and how it interprets the findings is not no-
tably progressive because, unlike physical science, which has its
own momentum—its own self-driven curve of development—
social science is by its nature deeply enmeshed in society's values
and ideologies. Here is an illustration. In *The Prehistory of Europe,*
author Patricia Philips emphasizes "homebody" archaeology—a
departure, according to a reviewer, from "older summaries, which

tended to emphasize the adventurers, explorers, and migrants of European history" (*Science*, October 31, 1980). In other words, the glamorous Scythians and horse nomads are out, and the place-bound tillers of the soil are in. A new picture of prehistoric Europe begins to emerge in the 1980s, not because new evidence calls for it, but because contemporary ideology demands it.

But hold on! Fashions change. Now, twenty years later, mobility is back. The study of great migrations, diffusing genes and culture, is again respectable. (See Marta Mirazón Lahr, "Wandering Genes," *Science*, September 22, 2000.)

Theoretical scientists promise people mystery and splendor—quarks and black holes, the frenzied birth of the universe. That's why they are esteemed. Applied scientists promise people power—faster painkillers and cars. That's why they are popular. By contrast, humanists promise neither. What they offer may provide a lilt to life, but quite as often they (historians and novelists of realism, in particular) do the opposite: offer the sad music of humanity, or sublime gloom and doom, as in Oswald Spengler's *The Decline of the West.*

The deep satisfaction of rigorous philosophical thinking is invisible to the public. Moreover, because of the rigor, the satisfaction cannot be widely shared even when the thinking process is clearly laid out. By contrast, the public can understand—or thinks it can understand—the conclusion of such thought: for example, there is no free will. Unfortunately, what is grasped is bad news. Why, then, should the public support philosophical humanists?

G. H. Hardy (pure mathematician) and Bertrand Russell (logician and philosopher) were close friends. Unlike most of us, they took such delight in rigorous reasoning that they did not mind the conclusion, however distressful. In the midst of an argument, Hardy said to Russell, "Much as I'll miss you, if I can find a logi-

cal proof that you will die within the next twenty-four hours I
should be glad." Russell replied, "But, dear Hardy, so should I!"

Wittgenstein, distinguished logician and philosopher, believed that knowledge isn't real unless it can be felt in the bones.
He discussed this matter with his student Norman Malcolm and
the student's wife as they walked down a narrow street in Cambridge, England. Wittgenstein complained, in particular, about
schoolchildren's understanding of the solar system—far too abstract, in his view. What can be done? How can a teacher make
the solar system more concrete and real? An idea occurred to
Wittgenstein, which he immediately put into practice. He asked
that Mrs. Malcolm continue to walk at a normal pace. She was
the sun. He asked Malcolm to run around his wife as the earth,
while he—the middle-aged professor—rushed madly around
Malcolm as the moon. The good citizens of Cambridge, though
they were used to the eccentric behavior of academics, were as-
tonished and got out of their way. (See Norman Malcolm, *Ludwig
Wittgenstein: A Memoir.*)

Can science destroy fond illusions? Alas, it can. Here is how
C. S. Lewis describes the planet Venus in his novel *Perelandra*, first
published in 1943, when it was still possible to give some cre-
dence to his account. And, to me at least, much of the magic of
that novel depends on the plausibility of its Venusian geography:

> There was no land in sight. The sky was pure, flat gold like
> the background of a medieval picture. It looked very dis-
> tant—as far off as a cirrus cloud looks from earth. The
> ocean was gold too, in the offing, flecked with innumer-
> able shadows. The nearer waves, though golden where
> their summits caught the light, were green on their slopes:
> first emerald, and lower down a lustrous bottle green,
> deepening to blue where they passed beneath the shadow
> of other waves.

Sadly, spacecraft exploration shows that Venus is more like hell than a sort of watery heaven.

The planet Venus has clouds of sulfuric acid, an air pressure that could crush a human being, and a temperature of 850 degrees. (The color scheme, however, approximates Lewis's vision.) "Should a visitor descend to the planet's surface, Venus at first would look like a fuzzy, cream-colored ball," said Brian Toon of NASA. "The sky is sort of a peach color. You don't see little clouds drifting by. You just sort of see a suspended, diffuse, pink glow. At night there are no stars."

Magasin (French) = storehouse of goods
Magazine = storehouse of knowledge

Both became popular in the early part of the nineteenth century—a peak of bourgeois achievement. Is it possible to have the one without the other? The modern university has been characterized as a department store or supermarket of knowledge. Students shop among its amply stocked aisles, picking up courses with the help of a thick catalog. The salad bar at some restaurants provides another analogy. Clients are encouraged to create their own mix. The problem with education—and with modern life, generally—is that few people know what to use for salad dressing. It is the dressing that gives integrity and character to the mix.

René Dubos, a distinguished microbiologist, was a towering leader of the environmental movement in the 1960s and 1970s. He became somewhat disillusioned, however, late in life—not with the goal of the movement, but with the intellectual preparedness of its ardent young supporters. He even thought that his own multidisciplinary approach to environmental problems was setting a bad example. He put it this way:

> When I retired . . . I was asked to teach in two universities. I seemed to be a big success. But I was a "big success" in

a way I found extremely dangerous. The students saw me, at the end of my life, working on very general problems and making observations about every discipline, be it social, medical, or scientific. Immediately they wanted to do the same thing, to come to grips from the start with problems on a worldwide scale, without being willing to work before thinking. Yet I'd tell them every day, "I want to stress that for forty years I was the most disciplined microbiologist possible . . ." But they simply wouldn't accept my explanation. I believe that from then on I began to feel that I was a bad influence on them. Because my courses were going too well, I gave up teaching and from then on gave no more courses of that sort. (*Science*, April 17, 1992)

Failure is more a fact of life in human beings than in other animals because we, unlike them, do periodically strive for perfection. Infants less than six months old already show strong aesthetic-intellectual yearnings. Years ago I read an account of an experiment that puts a small rubber ball in the infant's hand so that when she squeezes it an abstract shape appears on a screen, the shape changing with each squeeze until it approximates a circle. Well, it takes some doing, but the infant persists, despite repeated failures, until she breaks into a cherubic smile as if to say, "Voilà!—the circle of perfection."

My thought jumps to Einstein's manuscript on relativity, written in 1912 but never published. It shows his desire for perfection, even in literary style. "On each of the manuscript's oversized leaves, Einstein has crossed out words, jammed extensive inserts between the lines, and, in one case, drawn a slash through almost an entire page" (*New York Times*, March 15, 1996). Note the persistence, the repeated failures, and the final qualified success.

When we feel discouraged by our botched efforts, it helps to think of the infant and of Einstein. If we are at all ambitious, inevitably we fail far more often than we succeed. "Learning for success!" may be a good enough slogan for the professional schools, but liberal arts have higher aims. What, for example?

Well, wisdom, which Theodore de Bary, provost emeritus of Columbia University, defines as "learning how to endure failure" (*Education about Asia*, February 1996). Right. Yet somehow I can't imagine him, as provost, putting it in the university's brochure.

～

What is it like to attend a fair-sized class in which the professor doesn't know the students' names and doesn't encourage frequent give-and-take exchanges except in special, set-aside periods? Is it cold and impersonal, lacking in emotional rapport? One would think so. I am, alas, that professor, and I have just described my own class. Imagine my surprise, then, when a student accosted me to say, "Do you realize that you often pause in midsentence?" "Darn it," I muttered to myself, "another defect in my teaching technique, and this on top of not knowing their names." But the student continued: "When you pause and struggle to find the right word, do you realize that the entire class— well, maybe not the entire class, but it feels that way—moves forward to the edge of their seats in sympathy, *willing* you to find the right word—to succeed?" Wow! How wonderful that students should see their professor as performing some kind of high-wire act and themselves—their natural sympathy and intellectual engagement—as providing the safety net. No wonder canned lectures are no substitute for ones delivered in the flesh. Students want to see the *act* of thinking, and they want to feel that real failure—an experience so familiar to them—is always possible.

Of course, some students are bored. Where is the multimedia show? But more students than one might expect are remarkably willing to forgive their professor's lack of pedagogic technique provided that he takes pains (and pleasure) in reminding them of the existence of the True, the Beautiful, and the Good. Teaching, in the end, is that simple—and that difficult.

～

Being "up-to-date" in perspective or theoretical outlook may be essential in a professor of the sciences, but I am not so sure that it is as essential in a professor of the humanities. It may well be that the humanities professor's greatest contribution to his students' education lies in being "out-of-date," in being a creature of his time—a time that no young student has personally experienced—and so provide them with a difference of outlook that cannot be found in "cutting edge" journals or in the discourses of groovy young instructors. In English and cultural studies departments awash with deconstructionism and feminist theory, think how refreshing it is for the student to step into the classroom and hear the views of a scholar who is a positivist, or even a Christian humanist! Now that would be exposure to real difference—to another world, another time, another reality.

A good reason for reading the classics is their shock value. Who would have thought that there is a disquisition on farting in Augustine's *City of God?* As fallen creatures, Augustine asseverates, we fart from necessity and often beyond our control. Moreover, what comes out of us smells. Nevertheless, there is a hint of our pre-fallen state in that "some can from their bottom produce odorless notes so deliberately timed" that they seem to be "singing from that end, of all places."

The fall of totalitarian and authoritarian states has had one unfortunate consequence for me: I am no longer able to relax over *Soviet Life, China Reconstructs,* and *Free China Review* (Taiwan), with their pages filled with pictures of fat babies, rich harvests and gleaming tractors, apple-cheeked young pioneers and toothy ethnics. So, in desperation, I turn to *National Geographic* in the hope of finding Eden there. Sad to say, *National Geographic,* too, has succumbed to hard-hitting realism. Consider the contents of the August 1994 issue. Its cover story is "Lions of Darkness." Photographers who witnessed the prolonged death throes of an elephant as the lions clamped their teeth into its throat confessed to feeling a little queasy. Nevertheless, they depicted the horrors in loving detail. Elsewhere, they captured other assortments of painful death—for example, "Deadly Jellyfish of Australia"—in full color. The photo-essay "England's Lake District" sounds wholesome. I count on finding pictures of natural beauty there, and indeed I find two. The others are more in the spirit of our time: the village of Windermere strangled by motorcars, bracken ferns that give off deadly toxins, a close-up of a pop-eyed sheep being sheared by a pair of brutal-looking hands, a boy bent doubt in pain after a race, and so on.

What's wrong? Can it be that we have all become so sophisticated—so knowing—that we live in fear of being caught saying anything good about God's creation?

What is truth? Harvard's motto used to be *Veritas Christo et Ecclesiae* (Truth for Christ and the Church). It was eventually shortened to just *Veritas*. Harvard's crest used to show three books, one of which faced down to suggest the limitation of human knowledge. Eventually, this was changed so that all three books faced up, to show (I suppose) the boundlessness of human mental reach. However, it happens that God and *veritas* are closely linked: no God, no *veritas*. Truth is the degree that human beings can know God and his creation. Since human beings are made in God's image, knowledge of him and his handiwork is possible, though, of course, it cannot be complete. In the absence of a strong sense of something out there that can be known and is worth knowing, truth in time becomes merely stories we tell ourselves for consolation or power play. There are many such stories and one story is as good—as "true"—as another. Harvard's great discovery in the modern age is that books of knowledge are not written by God but by human beings—indeed, the best are written by Harvard men!

"He that increaseth knowledge increaseth sorrow." Not a likely logo for any university except, possibly, one determined to make minority students feel at home. How? An easy (cop-out) way is to heed Ecclesiastes and refrain from demanding of them any serious effort to increase their knowledge and experience. This means offering them courses on their own culture, taught by professors and administered by deans of their own ethnic background, in a milieu that reminds them of home, which means—if we are logical—a campus free of such unhomelike structures as libraries and high-tech labs. Surprising is not so much that minority students should make such irrational, self-defeating demands, for they have the excuse of youth and ignorance, but that university authorities should cater to them. Authorities seem more keen to assuage their feelings of guilt, accrued by past injustices done to African Americans, than to give their descendants the best possible education. And the best education is seldom easy for either faculty or students.

Geography

The idea of love, in Sumerian, seems to embrace the idea of geography. This is how S. N. Kramer puts it: "The Sumerian word for 'love' is a compound verb which seems to mean literally 'measure the earth,' 'to mete out a place'; just how this developed into the meaning 'love' is uncertain" (*The Sumerians*).

The Greek word *ethos*, by the fifth century B.C., was understood to mean "character." And this meaning is retained to our day: ethos, ethics, morality—character. But, according to Charles Chamberlain, *ethos* in Homer's time meant "the places where animals are usually found," "animal haunts or places." The shift in meaning to "character" probably went like this: Animals that are pastured in a certain place develop certain strengths and weaknesses—a set of habits, a character—thanks to the peculiarities of that place. Ethos and place are thus closely related. And *place* is of course a key term in geography. (See "From 'Haunts' to 'Character': The Meaning of Ethos and Its Relation to Ethics," *Helios*, vol. 11, no. 2, 1984.)

The reason Christopher Columbus was so eager to set sail in 1492 was that, according to Pierre d'Ailly's *Imago Mundi*, which Columbus held in high esteem, there were just 155 days left to humankind before the Apocalypse. If further evidence is required to show how remote Columbus's thought process was from ours, consider the following words in a letter he wrote to Ferdinand and Isabella in 1500: "I was not aided by intelligence, by mathematics or by maps. It was simply the fulfillment of what Isaiah had prophesied." (Simon Schama, "They All Laughed at Christopher Columbus," *New Republic*, January 6, 1992)

Envy is a fact of life, deeply embedded in human nature. It is the sin we are most reluctant to acknowledge in ourselves because, unlike pride, lust, avarice, and sloth, it implies inferiority. To be envious, we have to recognize a quality or possession in other people that we ourselves lack, and yet simultaneously deny that other people have it.

Envy can be directed at good looks, cleverness, wealth, social position, and so on. Yet, apparently, not at geography. So far as I know, Alabamans do not envy Californians—do not wish, as a people, to uproot themselves for a fairer and richer state. The envious rejoice in other people's misfortune. When an earthquake devastates California, Alabamans do not rejoice. Can it be that home places are truly unique and so cannot be compared and ranked? To Alabamans, their state offers a wealth of experience both good and bad that simply is not replicable in California or anywhere else.

Name-dropping. For a geographer, I suppose the names dropped would have to be place names. When I talk about myself, I try not to say, "Ah yes, as Lord Jebb of Britain said to me in 1950..." But I have not been able to forgo place-name-dropping. I do it even when no one is listening, as if to prove to myself that I've lived: "Ah yes, I played hide-and-seek in the rice fields of Sichuan, took numerous ferryboat rides across Sydney's fabulous harbor, stayed almost a week as the unwilling guest of the British government on the island of Malta, climbed over the stone fences of the Cotswolds, slept several nights in a partially sunken pleasure boat off the Atlantic coast of Panama, ate a bologna sandwich at the foot of Ayer's Rock, woke up to the sun illuminating the lunar landscape of Death Valley . . ."

Why is geography a strong school subject in England and Germany, and a weak one in the United States? One answer is that England and Germany were once imperial powers. As Germany's imperial ambitions increased, its government found it expedient to persuade the universities to accept geography as an academic subject. Geography was seen as a necessary tool in the making of wars—bloody wars and (in peaceful interludes) trade wars. Significantly, the schools in the United States that teach the most geography are the military and semimilitary schools of Texas.

Oceanographic mapping has made enormous progress since the end of the Second World War. So many new submarine mountains, ridges, and chasms have been discovered that scientists are hard pressed to come up with names. They have used the names of characters from J. R. R. Tolkien's fantasies and they have used the names of novelists. They have also used the names of musicians. Somewhere to the north of Hawaii lies a row of Musician Seamounts—from Strauss in the north to Mendelssohn in the south. There is a Bach Ridge and a Beethoven Ridge. There is also Mount Mozart. James Hamilton-Paterson comments in *The Great Deep:* "The presence of this random clutch of composers *engloutis* in the middle of Pacific wastes is a reminder of how much of the physical world [still] . . . belongs to the Western nations."

Non-Western nations do not have the power to name geographical features other than those within their own borders. A European or American scientist can offer to name a submarine feature for a non-Western nation, call one bulge on the ocean floor Mount Senghor, another Li Po Ridge. But that would be patronizing.

A snowflake, under the microscope, shows perfect design. Yet there is no designer. Likewise, though less perfectly, the hierarchical arrangement of settlements in the Middle West. Flying at night at an elevation of 30,000 feet, I can see below me a brilliant cobweblike arrangement of towns—a glittering tiara (the big town) surrounded by a ring of lesser towns, and beyond them a scattering of lights, and thence total darkness until the next set of lights comes into view. "You have flown, so I am sure you know what I mean," I say to students in my geography class. "You would think that a central intelligence—the federal government?—had designed it. But no. No one did. This thing of beauty is the consequence of myriad individual and small-group decisions operating under the push and pull of economic forces. Precisely how it came about is explained by the Central-Place theory, one of the few grand theories in the geographer's toolbox."

I present the theory and then stop. I can go further, of course, and press the vaguely disturbing point that design does not imply a designer and so lead the students, many of whom only want to know "where places are," into a theological quagmire from which there is no hope of deliverance.

People say, "We should live up to our heritage—our past or history." But with the exception of poet Theodore Roethke, they do not say, "We should live up to our geography—that geography places an obligation on us to be good or noble." Why the difference? Is it because of the belief that whereas history sanctions geography, geography merely influences history?

To geographers, refuge is clearly a geographical concept. Home is a refuge; a landscape can be a refuge too. Yet, to

Buddhists, a typical refuge is a good person or a sacred text
rather than the bodhi tree or a sacred river. And to Christians?
Christ on the cross and the Babe in the manger are two favorite
refuges for those who sorrow or are troubled in mind. Though I
am a geographer, my favorite refuges are more likely to be happenings than places. A holiday is a success if, unexpectedly, it
provides me with a happening to which I can withdraw when
I am in need of succor. Consider my trip to Colorado in 1995.
I appreciated the mountain grandeur, which has a way of palliat-
ing sorrow or disappointment by putting it in perspective. Yet
scenery was not enough for me. I also yearned for the significant
event. One afternoon during the Colorado tour, I found myself
waiting for my brother in the parking lot of a mining school. A
man came out of an office building carrying a jar that had a piece
of cardboard over the top. A wasp dashed crazily inside. The
man put the jar on a bench, removed the cardboard, and waited
for the wasp to escape. Somehow it couldn't manage. The man
returned to the building. A few minutes later, he came out again
and saw that the wasp had escaped. He picked up the jar and
went back to the building. The man had no idea that I watched
him. Even if he did, he couldn't have known that he had provided me with a refuge. And so even in the smallest gesture, we
are our brother's keeper.

Theological geography (after Hannah Arendt, *Men in Dark
Times*).
Paradise: "Right makes Might."
Earth: "Might makes Right."
Hell: "Wrong makes Might."

Some minds are relentlessly abstract. The English philosopher
G. E. Moore kept a journal in which he itemized "every walk he
ever took, and those walks he habitually took alone he characterized not geographically or topographically, but geometrically.
He would write that he had walked 'the parallelogram' or 'the

rectangle,' where someone else might have said he had walked, for example, to Granchester or around Parker's Piece." (Paul Levy, *Moore and the Cambridge Apostles*)

Country, neighborhood, world. "Ask not what your country can do for you but what you can do for your country." John F. Kennedy was criticized for expressing a sentiment that carried fascist undertones. What about "Ask not what your *neighborhood* can do for you but what you can do for your neighborhood"? Or "Ask not what the *world* can do for you but what you can do for the world"?

The last two sentiments are just fine. They are not controversial. A problem with the first sentiment is that a nation-state has guns. To put it another way, a nation-state is at the wrong scale, being neither small enough to arouse our compassion nor large and inclusive enough to justify unquestioning allegiance.

Geography and history are often coupled together, even though they differ widely in epistemological status. Geography is indispensable to survival. All animals, including American students who consistently fail their geography tests, must be competent applied geographers. How else do they get around, find food and mate, avoid dangerous places? History, in striking contrast, is an esoteric field of knowledge, and for that reason it plays only a small, indeed negligible role in the common tasks of life. It is not far-fetched to call animals geographers, but it is to call them historians. With animals and probably most human beings, knowledge of the past is folded wholly into present time and space—into geography, where the challenges of living lie.

Not only the individual but also society can survive in ignorance of its past. Indeed, a society can flourish without historical knowledge. India is a case in point. It has produced a civilization rich in myths and legends, cosmogonies and cosmologies, but not in the kind of accurate depiction of the past known to Europe and China. The Chinese take immense pride in their historical knowledge. But even the ultrachauvinists among them would hesitate to claim that their civilization is thereby superior. Indeed, the flow of high culture—Buddhism, outstandingly— was from India to China.

Geographers concentrate on peace and everyday life. Historians, by contrast, concentrate on war, and have done so since Thucydides set them an example. Consider the shelf upon shelf of history books about the American Civil War. I don't know of a single geography book on the subject. Now you know why history is more popular than geography. War with its rich cast of heroes and villains, politicians and generals, is exciting, whereas peace—the daily life of nameless folks—is boring.

If knowing how it felt to be alive at certain times in the past is a desideratum in historical geography, then the historical geographer has much to learn from the novelist. One such novelist is John Updike, whose *In the Beauty of the Lilies* is superb historical geography, except for one defect from a scholar's point of view: its principal characters could have existed but didn't. Updike's novel covers the period from 1910 to 1990—nearly the whole of the American century—and spans the continent, its principal locales being the Eastern seaboard, the West Coast, and the mountains of Colorado.

What can the historical geographer learn from it? First and foremost is the desire to experiment with overarching themes other than the changing landscape. Why not follow Updike and explore the decline of mainline religion and the rise of the image or media? These parallel and intermittently intertwined themes certainly affected American character and landscape in the twentieth century. The book starts with a Presbyterian minister losing his faith and ends with his great-grandson becoming the disciple of a guru in Colorado. The other theme with which the book starts is Mary Pickford making a movie in Garrett Mountain, New Jersey, not far from where the minister lost his faith. From there, it moves on to the rise of the movie industry in California and its challenge by television, and it ends with the glare of media on the besieged Colorado commune where the guru preached Day-of-Reckoning spirituality and savored, between-times, the bodies of his female followers.

Second lesson is in landscape description. Updike's landscapes come to life because they are experienced by ordinary people as they go about their business, and not framed and measured by an outsider eager to obtain material that can be written up. And landscapes are not just one-time affairs, but are experiences at different stages of life, sometimes after a lapse of years, such as when the heroine, who had become a Hollywood star, returned briefly to her hometown in Delaware. Geographers can be counted on to tell the reader how many drugstores there are in Garrett Mountain in 1920 and what they look like. But they seldom depict a place's passing mood and atmosphere, or penetrate building facades to describe what places look like on the *inside*: for example, what kinds of magazines are on display in a twenties drugstore?

Third lesson is the importance of providing adequate context for how people feel, think, and act. Historical geographers too easily forget the importance of *indirect* experience. What matters to an individual at a particular moment may not be his immediate surroundings, but rather what he happens to be reading in a magazine or hearing on the radio. The Presbyterian minister picks up Paterson's *Evening Times* from his porch. He withdraws gratefully to his study and reads. What are the headlines on that particular day in 1910? What is the local news? What sports are reported? What gripping events on the international scene make the front page? A cabdriver drives along a mountain road in Colorado in 1987 and turns on the radio. What news, ads, and music will he hear? Awareness of the media—printed and otherwise—reminds us that we are not only in place, but also in space, a space defined by events located close by and hundreds, perhaps thousands, of miles away.

Fourth lesson is sensitivity to language. Insensitivity makes any evocation of the past seem not right—inauthentic. How will

the language of a Presbyterian minister in 1910 differ from that
of a Hollywood star in 1951 (when both Gary Cooper and Clark
Gable turned fifty)—or, for that matter, from the language of a
fundamentalist guru in 1989? How did a schoolboy swear in
1920?

The last lesson is the necessity for authorial toil. What an
enormous amount of work Updike has put into his novel. I feel,
in the end, rather discouraged. Updike's talent is exceptional.
In addition, he worked hard. We can work hard too, but as a famous and well-off writer Updike can tap into resources that
geographers can only envy. In the acknowledgments, he thanked
no less than thirty-six individuals. He had thirty-six assistants!

Geography has curiously skipped the question of evil and,
with it, questions of morals and ethics that have been and still
are a central concern of both Eastern and Western philosophy.
A reason for this egregious neglect is geography's traditional
claim to being an earth science, rooted in geology rather than in
history or political philosophy. Inanimate rocks do not stir the
passions. But what about biogeography? Biogeographers do engage with the animate, but, interestingly enough, most of them
are plant geographers, and plants are not believed to have that
capacity to feel pain and happiness that raises moral issues.
Would more zoogeographers have helped? Not necessarily, for
human geography is a well-established field, and people certainly
feel. Yet, until well into the second half of the twentieth century,
human geographers managed to avoid morals and morality altogether, or just skirt around their edges.

Why? Various factors have contributed to the blindness. One
is a concept called environmental determinism that has held remarkable sway over geographical thought throughout Western
history. It treats people as it treats animals and plants, that is, as
essentially passive organisms that respond to rather than act on
reality, and hence are beyond (or below) good and evil. By the
early twentieth century, when geographers began to see people

as powerful agents of change, moral questions still failed to emerge, for the geographers of that time were mostly converts from geology and so tended to talk about human beings as though they were just another type of geological agent, like wind, water, and ice. When at last geographers took people seriously as culture bearers and powerful cultural agents of change, a triumphalist view of their story again buried moral issues, in particular the ill consequences of human action. "Sequent occupance" is an example of triumphalism. Popular among human geographers from the 1920s to the 1940s, it encourages one to see successive changes as inevitable progress: first forest or brush, then farm and village, then town, finally city and suburb.

A deeper reason for the neglect of moral questions by geographers is their indifference to events. Events are best left to historians. Wars, prominent in history books, are conspicuously absent in geography books. There is of course a geography of the American Civil War, but geographers have not written it. They prefer to map battlefields—the cool and static aftermath of an event—rather than confront the clash of beliefs and armies in which courage, cowardice, wisdom, stupidity, good and evil are likely to be displayed.

When I look at a contoured map I see beyond the cartographic convention to a mountain slope that may be too steep to climb. Reality, for me, is the mountain slope, not the wriggly lines called contours. When a physicist looks at a set of mathematical equations, what does he see? Curved space? But "curved space" is just a poetic manner of speaking, an image he conjures up for the benefit of the layman. To the physicist himself, there is no better handle on reality than the set of equations. There is no beyond—no going beyond the equations.

Societies that have a mapping tradition appear to experience the twin pull of practicality and imagination—science and art.

In some, art triumphs so that maps have little or no practical use and would not even be called "maps" under a strict definition. An example might be the pilgrim route maps and sand mandalas of Tibet, which were more mythology than geography. In others, outstandingly China, a greater balance was reached. Historically, Chinese maps strove for accuracy because they served pressing secular needs, such as military success, controlling floodwater, and establishing property boundaries. A remarkable example of early achievement were the silk maps of Hunan province, found in a tomb that dates back to about 150 B.C. They showed the locations of army installations and headquarters; they used color to distinguish different kinds of features and to provide evidence of scale. Given this early start in scientific mapping, how is it that China eventually fell so far behind the West?

One answer might be the intimate bond—the *too* intimate bond—between maps and landscape art. Chinese landscape painting flourished from the eleventh century onward. Many paintings portrayed idealized scenes of "mountains and rivers"; some were bird's-eye views of actual towns and the surrounding countryside. How should we classify them—as landscapes or as maps? It is plausible to say that they were both, that a fusion of genres occurred such that works motivated primarily by aesthetics could also be used to find one's way around town. But for this reason—though obviously not for this reason alone—the empirical-scientific movement in Chinese cartography failed to soar. Even maps of the nineteenth century, with their sinuous dragonlike rivers and hills in profile, remind viewers of landscape art. Another possible factor is the importance of words and calligraphy in Chinese civilization. Unlike Western practice, words—many of them!—accompanied Chinese landscape paintings and maps. These words or characters were themselves a genre of art. They did not detract from—indeed, they stimulated—the development of landscape painting. From the standpoint of the development of scientific cartography, however, the lengthy texts proved a drag, for they provided so much information that they

seemed to have obviated the need to present data using cartographic techniques alone.

Maps can be misleading because they don't—and can't—convincingly represent the seamier side of life. Consider United
States Geological Survey topographic sheets. Looking through
them, one might well conclude that all is well with America.
What can be amiss when forests are green, rivers and lakes are
blue, and settlements are either an eye-catching yellow or a
healthy pink, depending on the scale? Conveying rot and degra-
dation cartographically is difficult, perhaps impossible, because
maps use conventional signs, which exhibit pattern, and pattern
is by its nature aesthetic, whether it represents tulips or sewage
pits.

Bruno Zevi notes that whereas there are innumerable Jewish
writers, poets, and musicians, there is not one great Jewish archi-
tect. Even Solomon had to send to Tyre for the builders of the
Temple. ("Judaïsme et conception spatio-temporelle en art,"
Dispersion et Unité, no. 14, Jerusalem, 1975)

A place is made up of houses and streets and other material
things. All need to be maintained if they are to remain service-
able and attractive. How rarely we think of place as, equally, a
construction of language; and once it is so constructed, it too has
to be maintained, from time to time, by further applications of
language. Kenneth Grahame provides a convincing example in
The Wind in the Willows. Mole and the Water Rat are good friends.
Rat has entertained Mole in his delightfully cozy rowing boat.
Now it is Mole's turn to reciprocate the hospitality, but he is
ashamed of his house, which he regards as a "poor, cold little
place." Rat's response is to recreate his friend's house verbally and
with appropriate gestures. "So compact! So well planned!" He

sets to building a fire and gets Mole to dust the furniture, but Mole discovers a new source of shame: there is no food.

> "No bread!" groaned the Mole dolorously; "no butter, no—"
>
> "No *paté de fois gras*, no champagne!" continued the Rat grinning. "Ah, that reminds me—what's that little door at the end of the passage? Your cellar, of course! Every luxury in this house! Just you wait a minute."

Down Rat goes, and back he comes, a bottle of beer in each hand, and one under each arm: "Self-indulgent beggar you seem to be, Mole," he observed. "Deny yourself nothing. This is really the jolliest place I ever was in. Now wherever did you pick up those prints? Make the place so homelike, they do. No wonder you're fond of it, Mole. Tell us all about it, and how you came to make it what it is."

Words are integral to the Chinese making of place—especially the landscape garden. Words complete the garden. The eloquence of rocks and water, pavilions and balustrades seems muted and uncertain without the added eloquence and authority of literary texts. How a great garden is constructed is told in a mid-eighteenth-century novel called *The Story of the Stone.* The novel describes a distinguished family that was about to be honored by a visit of a daughter of the house, who also happened to be an imperial concubine. A special garden had to be built to accommodate such an august personage. The work was all done except for the inscriptions. The head of the family, Jia Zheng, and his guests came to take a look:

> "These inscriptions are going to be difficult," Jia Zheng said. "By rights, of course, Her Grace should have the privilege of doing them herself; but she can scarcely be expected to make them up out of her head without having seen any of the views which they are to describe. On the other hand, if we wait until she has already visited the gar-

den before asking her, half the pleasure of the visit will be lost. All those prospects and pavilions—even the rocks and trees and flowers will seem somehow incomplete without that touch of poetry which only the written word can lend a scene.

History

Many people seek to escape the horrors of the present age by envisaging an Eden or utopia long ago. I too periodically find relief in history, but what works for me is the awareness that however bad things are now, they were probably worse, overall, in the past. Here is an example. A knight, writing a letter to his humanist friend on October 1518, explained that life as an aristocrat left much to be desired:

> Do not envy me my life as compared to yours. Such is the lot of the knight that even though my patrimony were ample for my support, disturbances remain which give me no quiet. We live in fields and forests. Those by whose labors we exist are poverty-stricken peasants. The return is exceedingly sparse in proportion to the labor expended.... I must attach myself to some prince in the hope of protection. Otherwise every one will look upon me as fair plunder. But even if I do make such an attachment, hope is beclouded by danger and *daily anxiety.* The country itself is unsafe. We cannot go unarmed beyond two yokes of land. On that account we must have a large equipage of horses, arms, and followers, and all at great expense. We cannot visit a neighboring village or go hunting or fishing save in iron. (R. H. Bainton, trans., *Ulrich Von Hutten and the German Reformation*, 1937; emphasis added)

What was it like to travel between Paris and Bordeaux—a civilized part of Europe—as Arthur Schopenhauer and his father

did in January 1804? Rudiger Safranski gives the following account in *Schopenhauer and the Wild Years of Philosophy*:

> It rained continuously. The roads were sodden. Often fa-
> ther and son had to help move stones out of the way. On
> one occasion a wheel broke. They had to walk for miles to
> get help. There was interminable waiting at the staging
> posts. There was a shortage of horses. [Foodstuffs were
> hard to obtain.] Provisions were stolen from the carriage.
> Between Poitiers and Angoulême, marauding gangs were
> reported to be roaming the countryside. Locals warned
> against certain routes, but one could not be sure that this
> itself was not a trap.

I think of this passage as I wait at Chicago's O'Hare International Airport for a flight that is twice delayed. It helps me to
restore my equilibrium.

What might Madison, Wisconsin, be like if it were a European city around 1800? I know that what follows is fanciful, but
let me indulge myself anyway. Pillory and stocks take the place
of the fountain on Library Plaza. Students on their way to school
nonchalantly throw turnips and rotten cabbages at the bobbing
heads of the stockaded, their lips bleeding and their eyes swollen
under impact. Where the clock tower now stands, a gibbet dis-
plays two corpses in iron cages. A blast of wind down Bascom
Hill makes them swing and clang against each other. Leaflets are
handed out on State Street announcing the forthcoming execution of a notorious highwayman. A gallows is put up on Capitol
Square. Barricades are erected on the converging streets in anticipation of a large and rowdy crowd. Meanwhile, life goes on as
usual. A butcher emerges from the corner where Stop & Shop
Grocery now stands. He wrestles a steer to the ground, plunges
his knife into its belly, and slits it open. Steamy entrails and
blood pour out to join the river of filth that moves sluggishly in
State Street's central gutter. Citizens walk on wooden clogs elevated on circlets of iron to negotiate the street's squelchy, slith-

ery, pungently odorous surface. From Langdon Street come loud, drunken shouts. The students are gearing up for their annual high jinks. A group runs to catch a greased pig that squeals in terror as it rushes past fraternity row and the Armory. One burly fellow makes a flying leap, lands on the pig, but cannot hold on to it. Another gets hold of the pig's tail, pulling it off as the maddened animal surges violently toward the steps of Science Hall, where it runs smack into a phalanx of anatomy students waiting for it with their knives. The consorted plunge of steel into the pig creates a fountain gushing blood. One last ear-splitting squeal and the animal dies. Mangy, half-starved dogs, barking ferociously, converge in anticipation of a feast.

History also consoles for the opposite reason. Far from presenting an exotic—even bizarre—scene like the one I just described, it shows me a scene or event that is familiar, endearing, and timeless. Here is a favorite of mine. It is a letter that a Greek schoolboy of the second or third century A.D. wrote to his father:

> It was a fine thing not to take me with you to town! If you won't take me with you to Alexandria, I won't write to you or speak to you or say good-bye to you. If you go to Alexandria, I won't ever take your hand or greet you again. That is what will happen if you won't take me. Mother said to Archelaus: "It quite upsets him to be left behind." It was good of you to send me a present the day you sailed. Send me a lyre, now, I beg you. If you don't, I won't eat, I won't drink. That's that. (*Oxyrhyneus Papyri,* quoted by Iris Origo in *The Vagabond Path*)

How delightful to know that even in antiquity a child could play hardball with his father. It is also reassuring to know that time does not destroy all, that it can leave bits and pieces of human experience—not necessarily the grand or the heroic—for latecomers to enjoy.

"Those who don't remember the past are condemned to repeat it." The philosopher Santayana said something like that and
it is widely quoted. But like many such wise sayings, the opposite
is equally true. "Those who *remember* the past," one may well say,
"are condemned to repeat it." And isn't this more true, at least in
the literal sense? After all, we are what we remember: past injuries and humiliations, if we remember them, constitute our
present, with all their bitterness intact. What Santayana means
by remembering has to be something else: he surely has the cool,
objective, yet compassionate remembering of the historian in
mind. Only as historians of our past can we learn from the past
and free ourselves from it. Alas, whereas we are all good story-
tellers and myth makers, few of us—very few indeed—are good
historians.

Aesthetics

The root meaning of *aesthetics* (*aesthesia*) is "feeling." To feel is to
come to life—to be alive. Its opposite is *anaesthesia*, the deaden-
ing of the senses. Busy men and women tend to regard the aesthetic ("beauty and all that") as marginal or superficial, a hobby
that one might take up after money-earning work. Yet there is
nothing superficial about coming to life, drawn by the beauties of
the world and wanting to add to them. Human culture—everything from the well-turned phrase to great systems of thought,
from cosmeticized hair to great works of architecture—is a striving toward a keener, more shapely, more comprehensive and
comprehensible life.

"Tactile aesthetics," portentous and esoteric as it may sound,
refers to the most common and necessary of aesthetic experiences. The pleasures of being alive and our deepest sense of well-
being depend on cutaneous rewards that may come anytime,
anywhere: the coolness of a stone in the shade, the warmth of a
coffee cup, the smoothness of a baby's skin, the roughness of a
cobbled walk, the fat kiss of raindrops, the feel of the carpet

under the desk as you slip your stockinged foot out of your moccasin and brush your foot over its plush surface, and even "the slippage of the inner surface of the sock against the underside of your foot, something you normally only get to experience in the morning when you first pull the sock on" (Nicholson Baker, "Shoelace," *New Yorker,* March 21, 1988).

Fragrance, no matter how desirable, turns offensive when it is too strong. Music, no matter how heavenly, becomes pain when it is too loud or goes on for too long. What about visual beauty? Can we be put off by too much visual beauty in our homes and cities, or in a landscape?

We speak of the *savor* of life. With permanent loss of smell and taste, as can happen in a head injury, what's the point of living? Taste for sex weakens too, so much does sexual arousal, like food arousal, depend on odor. Can CDs and pictures and odorless landscape gardens really make up for the loss?

"Is it the essence of the artistic way of looking at things that it looks at the world with a happy eye?" Wittgenstein asks. Happiness is living more fully: eyes flooded with the harmonious lines of a landscape, ears filled with the sweetness of melody, mind stirred by the eloquence of an argument. A happy person has something to offer—his happiness. Why are the young able to impress their elders? They have beauty, which is often simply "the bloom of happiness," says Emile Chartier in *On Happiness.*

Between the second and third movement of Beethoven's Ninth Symphony, a young couple moved into the seats next to mine. During the adagio the young man noisily unwrapped peppermints for his girlfriend. And when, in the last movement, the solo quartet and chorus sang

Wer ein heldes Weib errungen
Mische seinem Jubel ein!

(He who wins a noble woman,
Let him join our jubilee!)

the couple smooched. And yet, weren't they more in tune with
the spirit of Beethoven and Schiller than I who sat alone, shrinking into my seat in distaste, eyebrows knitted in anger?

E. M. Forster says in *Two Cheers for Democracy* that the reason
he seldom attends concerts is that the audience is so ugly: "A
classical audience is surely the plainest collection of people anywhere assembled for any common purpose; contributing my
quota, I have the right to point this out." In a classical concert,
the audience has to concentrate on the music if only to dim its
awareness of circumambient human ugliness. In a rock or rap
concert, by contrast, the audience is young and handsome; it is
the music that is barely worth listening to. Hence, not surprisingly, people tap or gyrate, using the throbbing sound to advertise and magnify their own beauty.

Ballet is an especially challenging art because it has to compete with the *natural* grace of human movement. Children tum-
bling over monkey bars and riding skateboards already provide
much aesthetic pleasure. Why should I pay to see a ballet unless
it offers me far more vitality and grace than that which is avail-
able to me in any playground?

Children may be naturally graceful in posture and movement,
but their untrained voices are another matter—shrill and raucous
when excited, monotonic in recitation—compared with which
adult voices, except in altercation, are pleasing. This must be another reason why children should be seen but not heard.

During National Handicapped Week I witnessed a square dance performed by paraplegics in their wheelchairs outside the Social Sciences Building at the University of Minnesota.

The master of ceremonies—a man of sound body—made a brief announcement to a thin gathering of curious noon-hour students. He turned on the music and the wheelchairs swirled energetically over the pavement, bumping into each other now and then.

I do not recall ever seeing anything quite so unintentionally cruel. Victims of paralysis do not dance well. Their frenetic movements looked ridiculous alongside hale and loose-limbed youngsters who, by just standing there watching, were pictures of grace.

But what about the ability of movement as such to empower, regardless of whether it is done especially well? "There is a story told in *Treblinka* by Jean-Louis Steiner about a dancer standing naked in line waiting for her execution in the concentration camp. A guard tells her to step out of line and dance. She does, and carried away with her own authoritative action and with her individuality she dances up to the guard, takes his gun and shoots him." (Philip Hallie, *The Paradox of Cruelty*)

Daily life is made up of social ballets, performed with routine competence. One such ballet threatens to fall apart but doesn't, thanks to a last-minute, inspired rescue. Lunch is arranged in honor of a colleague who is about to take a two-year leave. After it, we rise from the table, shake his hand, wish him well, and tease him about having to surrender his parking space. We give him a final pat on the back. In a film, the scene fades at this point. In real life, however, we make our way to the coatrack, pick up our overcoats, and straggle to the elevator, where we meet again, this time unplanned, and wait awkwardly in each other's presence without a prepared script, until one person has to wit to say, "Such ragged endings are the stuff of real

life." With this remark he saves the appearance, reconverts life
into art.

All social events are occasions for ceremony. Such was the
tenet of late-nineteenth-century aesthetes. Hence it would not
do to be late. All entrances are "grand" entrances, and it would
not do to take leave at the door without a gracious remark or
flash of wit. Ballet and the theater are models to strive for even in
ordinary human exchange. Now, is this why, as social events become increasingly informal and slack in the twentieth century,
I find pleasure in the precision and formality of machines and
even in the scientific paper?

In 1946, I—a boy almost wholly ignorant of Chinese theater—attended the Peking opera in Shanghai. The famous
singer-actor Mei-lang Fang was to appear. It was rumored to be
his last performance, for he was nearly fifty years old, in poor
health and in poor shape. He had acquired a pot belly and could
hardly hope to sustain his young female roles much longer. But
could he do it even in 1946? The orchestra began to play; the
spectators fell silent. A male actor called out, "Young lady, enter!"
There was a rustling of the bamboo curtain and the young lady
(Mei-lang Fang), still behind the curtain, responded with a pierc-
ingly high note. Could art triumph over sex, age, and debility?
Was I really going to see a willowy young woman? Incredibly, I
did, such was the human need—and power—to conquer nature.

In 1950 I went to a play (Molière's *Le Misanthrope?*) performed
by the Comédie Française. My French wasn't really up to understanding the rapid dialogue and my meager experience of the
theater didn't prepare me to appreciate the subtleties of classical
acting. What I do recall from that evening, I am a bit ashamed to
confess. It was the feeling of excitement as the lights began to

dim; the way the chatter faded to silence and then, breaking into that silence, three thuds, made as though with a felt-wrapped hammer pounding the floor; the stately rise of the curtain, corresponding with the rising expectation in the darkened hall, to reveal the illuminated stage. To me, these moments possessed something of the raw power and mystery of a Beethoven overture. What followed—the patter of speech in a social setting—could only be a letdown.

"The poor in a state are like shadows in a picture; they create a necessary contrast, which humanity sometimes bemoans, but which does honor to the intentions of providence" (P. Hecquet, *La Médicine, la chirurgie et la pharmacie des pauvres* [Medicine, Surgery, and Pharmacy of the Poor], Paris, 1740).

Paris is one of the world's sophisticated cities where a sprinkling of the poor can drive up real estate prices. Rich Parisians, when they move into a neighborhood, want at least a few working-class families to stay, for they add color and picturesqueness to the neighborhood. It is pleasing for the rich to take their poodle out for a stroll and see a father on his bike, a baguette tied to the handlebar and a little boy wedged in the bucket seat behind. Workers and their families are part of the native fauna, no more to be driven out than the squirrels and pigeons, provided, of course, there aren't too many of them.

Why do we look at the armless Venus de Milo with pleasure rather than in horror? Isn't this the most striking difference between art and life?

In 1972 a madman damaged the eyebrow of Michelangelo's *Pièta* with a hammer. It became instant world news, featured on the front page of the national papers of the United States, Britain, France, Italy, and even India. The news completely over-

shadowed body counts in the Vietnam War. How pitifully dis-
posable and valueless young soldiers were compared to a work
of art. Here is another example. As a real human being with an
immortal soul, I am no doubt more valuable and, indeed, more
complex than any mere fictional character can possibly be. Yet,
whereas only a few pages (at the most optimistic count) have
been written about me, "since 1780, some 25,000 books, essays,
articles, contributions to critical and learned colloquia, doctoral
dissertations, have been produced on the true meanings of
Hamlet" (George Steiner, *Real Presences*).

The Italian author Natalie Ginzburg says in *The Little Virtues*
that there was a time when she concentrated on "gray, squalid
people and things" to write about. She sought out "a contemptible
kind of reality lacking in glory." One day, in her town, she saw a
"hand-cart being pushed through the street and on it was a huge
mirror in a gilded frame. The greenish evening sky was reflected
in it." As she stopped to watch, she felt that "something extremely important had happened" and was inexplicably happy.
Ginzburg tried to introduce that image into one of her stories,
but could not quite succeed. Nevertheless, this brief encounter
with the gilded mirror convinced her that unless she occasionally
introduced a touch of splendor into the lives she portrayed, her
realism was untrue to experience.

If William Blake can see the world even "in a grain of sand,"
then nothing is to him dismissible—unworthy of notice. The
trick, he might say, lies in paying proper attention. But paying
proper attention takes time and energy. We prefer diamond to
sand because with sand *we* have to do nearly all the work if it is
to seem interesting, whereas with a sparkling diamond *it* does
most of the work. The same line of argument applies to people.
Without doubt all human beings are potentially interesting, but
with some we have to work hard to find just what it is that makes

them so. When we do find this buried quality, we tend to congratulate ourselves for clever digging and charitable persistence rather than the person who possesses the quality.

My sister sends me a calendar from Taiwan every year. Each has a different theme: flowers, wildlife, gardens, rocks and minerals have appeared in the past. The colored photographs are nothing special, but pleasant enough to look at when one is too tired to take in anything else. This year the theme of the calendar is children. Good. I expect another pleasant half hour looking at the little ones. But no. Pictures of children are not relaxing in the manner that pictures of animals and rocks are. Why? One reason is the desire and anxiety that subtly distort many faces. The other is that, contrary to sentimental expectation, quite a few children are just not pretty, but plain, even ugly. *Ugly* is not a word I would apply to minerals. *Bizarre* perhaps. Plants, likewise. As for animals, I do find some—horned toads, snakes, orangutans—repellent. Why? Is it because animals, being sentient and capable of emotion, invite moral, and not just aesthetic, judgment?

One child out of 8 million children in this country is afflicted by a disease called progeria. The sufferer ages so rapidly that by the time the child is six he looks like a wrinkled dwarf, hairless and toothless, some three times older than his mother. What is it like to be such a child? Is parental love, which feeds (in part) on the apple-fresh cuddliness of the young, up to the challenge? Apparently yes. It shows how human beings can heroically rise above the message of the senses.

Are we less tolerant of human deformity than we were in the past? "In Renaissance Italy, the Lords of Ferrara and the Popes of Rome kept their houses full of absurd and sometimes very repul-

sive specimens of humanity," writes Enid Welsford in *The Fool*.
Can you imagine the Rothschilds and the Kennedys keeping
dwarfs in their households? No, they want to be surrounded by
Beautiful People—the brightest and the best.

Too bad that Iranian women have to wear the purdah, hiding
all parts of their body but the eyes, for many, being young, are
quite lovely. One can tell by looking at the eyes. On the other
hand, America would be even more beautiful if it adopted a dress
code (such as the purdah) for its aged citizens. I say this because
Madison's State Street, normally filled with comely college
youths, is in summer the haunt of septuagenarians and octogenarians seeking to escape Florida's torrid heat. They dress
minimally, flaunting their creased necks, spindly legs and arms,
and clawlike feet with toenails painted scarlet (in the case of
women) in a sort of in-your-fact dare.

Ugliness is at the surface; underneath is beauty. This is a common Western viewpoint—a noble one. Thus Socrates, though
plain, is wise. Frankenstein's monster is ugly outside but full of
warm human sentiment inside. The frog is really a prince. Christ
may be the outstanding exception. Under the idealizing influence of classical antiquity, he is often depicted as good-looking.
Still, Christ's outward appearance is as a coat of rags compared to
who he really is. What about beauty? Is it a cover for corruption
and evil? There I suppose the outstanding example is Lucifer.
Even in his fall, he has retained his archangelic shell, making him
all the more dangerous.

"What really matters is a person's inner beauty." But we don't
mean that literally, as the biologist J. B. S. Haldane does. He
once wrote: "It was not until I had attended a few postmortems
that I realized that even the ugliest human exteriors may contain
the most beautiful viscera, and was able to console myself for the

facial drabness of my neighbors in omnibuses by dissecting them
in my imagination."

Plato, in his myth of the cave, suggests that we are creatures
of the cave, comfortable with shadows and illusions, and unable
to bear the brightness of reality or truth, which is symbolized
by the sun. To moderns like Nietzsche and Eliot, the amount of
reality that human beings can bear is also limited. But the reality
or truth they have in mind is not something overpowering and
splendid like the blazing sun. Rather, it is something dark and
ugly—an offense to the spirit. As Nietzsche famously said, "We
possess art lest we perish of the truth." Art may be a lie, but it
is a beautiful lie, and our salvation. What a radical change in the
conception of reality this is. And how depressing.

"Anyone who keeps the ability to see beauty never grows
old," said Kafka. I like the idea until I realize that it applies not
only to me, an old man who delights in the vigor and beauty of
bubbling streams, but also to me, a dirty old man who salivates
over the bodies of the young.

Frustrating, isn't it, that we can depict human ugliness with
ease (even a young child can draw a credible monster), but we
can depict human beauty only with great difficulty? It doesn't
help that the most beautiful face—at least, the most beautiful
female face—is the average face, according to a study reported
by *Science* (April 20, 1990). The average face is hard to envisage
and harder still to draw. What about the male face? Consider
Michelangelo's *Moses*. It is in no sense average, and yet is strik-
ingly handsome. Do we judge male beauty by a different standard—do we think that what matters there is character and
force? And does this mean that it should be a little easier to draw
a handsome male face than a beautiful female one?

Bridget of Sweden (1303–73): "If we saw an angel clearly, we should die of pleasure."

Folk art does not appeal to me. Folk life does. High art appeals to me. High life does not. Classical ballet, yes; Latvian folk dance, no. I suppose my biases are influenced by the notion of work. Sweat and toil lie behind folk life, but not behind folk art. By contrast, sweat and toil—a sense of total dedication—lie behind high art, but obviously not behind high life.

I see erotic vitality in Chinese paintings of fishes and stallions and cannot help wondering what masterpieces would be given the world if Chinese artists had turned their imagination and skill to depicting the human nude, as Western artists have done. What would the Chinese rendition of a naked man or woman be like? Would the former have the sensual charge of a rearing horse, the latter the grace of a leaping carp?

Chinese artists have turned a blind eye to the darker and less respectable sides of life—dirt and decay, suffering and death, the exigencies of the body. Their tradition would not have allowed them to depict varicose veins and dirty feet, as Caravaggio did in Europe. And Caravaggio could do so because his art came out of centuries of close attention to thieves on the cross and blood-stained Christs. Rembrandt's *Slaughtered Ox* is totally beyond the pale of the Chinese artistic imagination. Equally beyond it is the defecating dog that Rembrandt saw fit to put in his morally uplifting picture *The Good Samaritan*. Chinese artists portray live birds and vigorous plants, as Western artists do, but Western artists do something else: fruits and flowers ("still lives") that are emblems of decay.

The workplaces of Chinese and Western artists differ markedly. Chinese artists have always believed that their environment must be aesthetically just right to support their artistic endeavor. By contrast, Western artists make little fuss over the quality of their workplace other than the lighting. Western art can make severe physical demands on its executor, who, for this reason, may need to have the muscles of a construction worker, the agility of an athlete, and the tolerance for disorder of a child. Think of Michelangelo on his back, high up on the scaffold, painting the ceiling of the Sistine Chapel, in the midst of dust and dripping paint. I can't imagine a Chinese artist exposing himself to such sustained labor and indignity. He would say that no great artwork can possibly come out of such a stressful and disordered setting.

Why is Chinese painting so deficient in the portrayal of light? Is it because China lacks a theology of light—of God as Light? Chinese artists are acclaimed for their sensitivity to nature, but where are the stars, night scenes, sunrise or sunset? Has a traditional Chinese artist ever tried to present vapor dancing in shafts of afternoon light, the glowing face of a happy child, leaves glistening after a shower, the sheen of steel, the shimmering heat of noon in summer?

Except in the auditory sphere, nature is a match—often more than a match—for art. Consider the texture of human skin or a rose petal. Can any manufactured surface reward the tactile sense more? The perfumer's art produces exquisite scents. But are they really superior to nature's? As for sight, we feast on great works of art, yet in their power to enchant, nature's works can hold their own: Michelangelo's *David* is matched by Davids who strut the streets of Florence, and the best landscape paintings in the world evoke an aesthetic response no more intense than that obtainable from nature. Sounds are another matter. Even nature's best—whispering pine, bubbling brook, the nightingale in full-throated song—can hardly compete, musically, with the simplest human tune, much less the *Pastoral* Symphony.

Here are three impassioned modern testimonies to the miraculous power—the supremacy—of music. Cellist Pablo Casals, at age ninety-three, said that music filled him "with awareness of the wonder of life, with a feeling of the incredible marvel of being a human being." Anthropologist Claude Lévi-Strauss declared that music is the supreme mystery of humanity. The philosopher Wittgenstein confessed to a friend that the slow movement in Brahms's Third Quartet had pulled him back from the brink of suicide. Have such compliments ever been directed at a painting or sculpture? Architecture ("frozen music") may have such power. I can imagine someone saved from suicide when he entered, by chance, a serenely or sublimely beautiful building.

George Bernard Shaw said disapprovingly of Mozart that "he put his raptures of elation, tenderness, and nobility into the mouth of a drunken libertine, a silly peasant girl, and a conventional fine lady." Shaw's criticism used to make sense to me. There was a time when I found Mozart's operas hard to take because of these jarring juxtapositions. But I now see differently. Maybe Mozart was making the theological point that "ordinariness" is superficial, that buried in every ordinary human being is a spirit that not only yearns for beauty but also is capable of creating it.

"I have no ear for music, a shortcoming I deplore bitterly," wrote Vladimir Nabokov in *Strong Opinions*. In a concert performance, rather than attend to the music, he found himself visually enthralled by "reflections of hands in lacquered wood, a delinquent bald spot over a fiddle." Does strength in one mode of perception tend to weaken strength in other modes? Does one exceptional talent curtail the development of another? Mozart had no eye for landscape. Many mathematicians have no ear for poetry. As for the rest of us, we are the fortunate ones who, unburdened by any special perceptual strength or talent, are free to enjoy multimodally. Receiving much, we give little, not from meanness, but because we have little to give.

Intellect

I like to invigilate exams despite the burden of having to grade them later, because I derive a powerful aesthetic pleasure from watching students think. To me, no facial expression, no posture is more attractive. I feel privileged to be watching an event that is extremely rare—perhaps even unique—in the universe.

The intellect doesn't rank high in human estimation, according to Montaigne. In support of his view, he quoted from *On the Nature of Things* by Lucretius: "The first distinction that ever existed among men, and the first consideration that gave some pre-eminence over others, was in all likelihood that of beauty. They divided the land and gave to each man in proportion to his beauty, strength, and intellect; for they prized beauty and esteemed strength.'" What happened to the "intellect" in the triplet? It was just quietly dropped.

You check in on the baby to see whether it is all right. You expect it to be asleep, but no, its eyes are wide open. What can the baby be thinking of, alone and in the dark? For the first time you are profoundly aware of being in the presence of an independent and unfathomable personality.

Small children, being true intellectuals, disdain small talk. I met Blake McGreevy (age three) in a dark corridor of the Social Sciences Building at the University of Minnesota. After the briefest acknowledgment of my existence, he plunged into a discourse on dinosaurs. In case I wasn't getting the picture, he opened his lunch box and showed me a rubber model. At this point, his eyes fell on some cookies, and for a tense moment I wondered whether the young intellectual was about to be derailed by mere bodily appetite. But no, he continued.

The great physicist Hans Bethe, when he was five years old, said to his mother while they were taking a walk, "Isn't it strange that if a zero comes at the end of a number it means a lot, but if it is at the beginning of a number it doesn't mean anything?"

At age five, I could do simple sums. Perhaps even a talented chimpanzee could do as much. But neither of us, even in our wildest dreams, would have found the position of zero worth puzzling over. Therein lies the difference between intelligence and divine intelligence.

Seven-year-old Michael, discussing the possible infinitude of the universe with his teacher, says: "I don't like to think about the universe without an end. It gives a funny feeling in my stomach. If the universe goes on forever, there is no place for God to live, who made it" (Gareth Matthews, *Philosophy and the Young Child*). The chances are good that Michael will grow up to be an astrophysicist or cosmologist. He will then, with the most refined logic and computations, try to demonstrate that the universe is finite. We shall see a mature and objective intelligence at work, yet the thesis itself may have its roots in the "funny feeling" of a child.

You might say that Michael has a closed mind: young as he is, he is not open to "the universe without an end." But isn't this a characteristic of creative individuals? Consider Einstein. His mind, averse to the idea that nature's laws are fundamentally statistical, seems closed to certain conclusions in quantum mechanics. One shouldn't be surprised, for a major function of the mind is to delimit and define—that is, close off. It is life that is disorientingly and distressfully open; hence, the constant tension between life and mind.

Tiger Woods, at age twenty-four, is often described by sports commentators as a golf genius and the greatest golfer ever. At age two, he putted with Bob Hope on *The Mike Douglas Show*; at age five, his fans requested autographs that he was too young to know how to sign; while his grade-school contemporaries drew pictures of racing cars and robots, Tiger sketched the trajectories of his iron; he was only eight when he won the Junior World Championship (*New Yorker*, August 21 and 28, 2000). We have all heard of music, math, chess, and even poetry prodigies. But an authentic golf prodigy, with the genius showing at a very early age, is new. It suggests, as a chess prodigy does, how specialized a great talent can be. This is in striking contrast with another kind of genius, which is able to emerge only against a broad and deep background of knowledge and experience. Charles Darwin is the outstanding example. Can one be a prodigy in biology? Or in philosophy? Conceivably, the boy Kant could have come up with the idea of the categorical imperative, but such an idea would be empty without detailed and systematic exemplification.

Almost all young children are intellectuals. They keep asking why. They are constantly experimenting. Their high-powered imagination produces refreshing poetry and art. If these gifts of mind continued undiminished and even enhanced into maturity, the world would be made up exclusively of artists, thinkers, and scholars. Fortunately, nature has made sure that this doesn't happen. At about age seven, children suddenly become social beings, bent on communicating with other children. To do so successfully, they must stop raising original (largely unanswerable) philosophical questions and they must curb the originality of their speech for something more readily shared and understood.

After a few years of this intense socializing with peers, children may want to return to their earlier intellectual bent, but most don't, because by then nature has thrown up another barrier— sex. The mind's development is once more set aside, this time in favor of sexual congress and baby talk.

Increasingly, scientists believe that the human brain evolved in response to the challenge of coping with slow-maturing children rather than, as previously thought, the challenge of making tools (*Science*, September 27, 1991). Even now, understanding social relations rather than physical reality consumes the bulk of the mental energy of chimpanzees and human beings. Only in the lab, under persistent human prodding, do chimpanzees puzzle over symbols and symbolic relationships. Only a few men and women in any society take time to wonder, abstractly, how nature or society works.

Western civilization has freed its mental energy, to a unique degree, from the task of sorting out social relationships. No longer forced to please one's maternal great uncle with the right sort of deferential gesture, or to decide what kind of gift to send to a cousin twice removed, more and more Westerners, from the seventeenth century onward, can undertake an impersonal interest in the external world. The result is a vast gain in scientific knowledge and a substantial loss in knowledge of social distinctions and, with it, a loss in the variety of kinship terms. I am willing to bet that the village headman is a subtler student of status hierarchy than is the chief of protocol at the U.S. State Department.

Here is an additional gloss. I have lost the reference and the details have grown vague in my mind, but the gist of the following story is true. In the 1960s, the American motorcar industry reluctantly concluded that the traditional factory system, in which each worker was treated like a machine part doing dull repetitive tasks, was demoralizing and inefficient, and that the

Swedish system of cooperative work in small teams was better. A select group of American workers was sent to Sweden to see how they liked the Swedish system. They liked it at first, but the novelty soon wore off, and they decided in the end that they actually preferred the duller American way. How come? Well, the greater technical challenge of the Swedish system was insufficient to ward off boredom. Meanwhile, the American workers missed what they really liked about work in America—the camaraderie of breakfast before work and of beer after work, an essential element of which was bitching! There was also the fun of factory politics, dissing the foreman, planning strikes at the local union, and so on. In other words, the satisfaction of work lies in the human relationships, including contestations and confrontations, outside of work.

In a cynical mood, I wonder whether this isn't true even at the university. In theory, work at the university is all-engrossing. One is, after all, doing research, pioneering new fields. In actuality, much research even at the university is fairly routine, even tedious, and adds little to basic knowledge. Faculty members know that campus politics can be more challenging—and certainly more rewarding.

Frederick the Great (1712–86) was an enlightened philosopher-king who, however, had little respect for the intelligence of ordinary people. He thought that only 200,000 out of 16 million Frenchmen (1.25 percent) had reasonably good minds. The rest were more like animals. "Men are not made for truth," he wrote to Voltaire. "I see them as a troop of stags in a great lord's park, they have no other function than to stock and restock the enclosure."

Frederick admired the great thinkers of his time and sought their company at every turn. But he was also suspicious of them. Great minds could be greatly intolerant. When Pope Clement XIV banished the Jesuits—the bête noire of philosophes—Frederick did not follow suit. "You accuse me of being too tolerant," he wrote d'Alembert. "I glory in this failing, would it were so that one could only reproach sovereigns for such faults." (Giles Mac-Donogh, *Frederick the Great*)

Mark Twain is reported to have said that genius is 1 percent inspiration and 99 percent perspiration. This sounds reassuring because we can all buckle down to hard work when necessary. But what's the good of hard work without the 1 percent inspiration that is beyond our beck and call? Absent the yeast of inspiration, the dough may attain mass but it will remain dough—a burden on the spirit.

The genius is someone who can derive powerful generalizations out of limited (and perhaps even biased) data: for example, Einstein, whose store of experimental data was surely no greater—and its quality no better—than that of his learned colleagues; or a child prodigy who, from a limited sample of life experience obtained more or less by chance, produces a poem that speaks to all.

In an interview with the famous anthropologist Claude Lévi-Strauss, the principal purpose of which was to discuss his work, he said wistfully: "Although I am going to talk about what I have written, my books and papers and so on, unfortunately I forget what I have written practically as soon as it is finished" (*Myth and Meaning*).

Well, there is intellectual advantage to forgetting. In a sense, we write in order to forget. Writing gives us that advantage over nonliterate people who have to carry the accumulated knowledge and misinformation of their tribe in their heads. They don't have the luxury of "cleaning the drawers" periodically and moving on to other things.

I used to take only one cup of coffee at the University Club. Now I take two. "Coffee is getting weaker," I say. "No," friends tell me, "the coffee remains the same but you need more of it—more stimulants to keep going." A pity that this is not true of intellectual fare. Do I now need to consume two books a week rather than one? And can I claim that now only a book with the punch of *The Critique of Pure Reason* will keep me awake and alert?

Thinking, which requires withdrawal from sensory awareness and society, is treated with suspicion in almost all cultures. It is also suspect for raising questions to which there are no answers, or to which the answers contradict society's revered norms. People who think are widely regarded as crazy (having taken leave of their senses) and as potential troublemakers.

One Inuit woman was overheard to say in a righteous tone, "I never think." Another woman complained of a third because she was trying to make her think and thus shorten her life (Jean Briggs, *Aspects of Inuit Value Socialization*).

An American working-class father sees his son reading. He doesn't like it. "He doesn't know why it makes him nervous to see the kid read. Like he's plotting something. They say you should encourage it, reading, but they never say why" (John Updike, *Rabbit Is Rich*).

Contrary to widespread belief, Americans worship brainpower. In this country you are free to boast about such advantages as wealth and physical prowess—even your good looks—but the sky will fall if you so much as hint that what distinguishes you from others is your superior brain. For, unlike the other claims, which still leave you human, the claim to a superior brain is a claim to being an equal of the gods. When Muhammad Ali says "I am the greatest," we smile indulgently. Imagine physicist Richard Feynman saying that!

The boxer is an entertainer, and so is the rock star. Americans are willing to pay extravagantly for entertainment. They are apparently also ready to give their entertainers adulation. I say "apparently," because Americans know full well that, in the final analysis, *they* are the boss; they are the ones who insist on being entertained—either that, or back to the poor neighborhoods from which many of the athletes and singers come. As for intellectuals and thinkers, they will never be paid at a level commensurate with their contribution to society. They will never receive adulation. They cannot—must not—be elevated, for they already occupy seats on Olympus. In a populist egalitarian society, intellectuals and thinkers do something unforgivable. They presume to impart new knowledge—to teach.

Sometime in the turbulent 1970s, I saw a photograph in *Science* magazine of young men and women lined up in front of what looked like a factory or a warehouse. Their mouths were open and their fists were raised. Another protest, I thought. But no. They were shouting "Eureka!" for the same reason that Archimedes did some two thousand and two hundred years ago. They had just made an important scientific discovery. How is it that we students of society almost never experience this level of joy? And is this why we, in envy, declare that there is nothing to discover—that even physical reality is social construction?

French mathematician Alain Connes won the Field medal (the top honor in mathematics) in 1983. In 2001 the Swedish Academy of Sciences awarded him the prestigious Crawford Prize. Not only did Connes invent new tools for probing math's most famous unsolved problem, the Riemann hypothesis, but these tools have also proven useful to theoretical physicists. What is it like to read the works of a man whose mind is as penetrating as it is original? Well, one reviewer of Connes's book *Noncommutative Geometry* said that it produced in him a "feeling of intense jubilation" (*Science*, February 2, 2001).

A feeling of intense jubilation! Even a mathematical dork like me, whose exposure to this achievement is so indirect (by way of a news report), can feel a vicarious glow of happiness. More. For a brief moment, I am convinced that God is in his heaven and all is well with the world.

~•

Benjamin Franklin said we are a nation of "happy mediocrity." I just hope we never become a nation of resentful mediocrity.

~•

I have heard it said that clever people are easily bored, but also that they are never bored. I suggest that the latter is closer to the truth. My case is supported by the attitude of Y. R. Chao, a clever man and a distinguished linguist who enjoys parties and gives the impression of always being attentive. How does he avoid boredom? Well, Chao listens because people, in fact, have something to say. But if their talk is empty, he still listens—this time as a technical linguist attending to the medium rather than to the message.

~•

Cathleen Morawetz of the Courant Institute of Mathematics at New York University was asked whether she didn't worry about her young children when she was at work. The questioner no doubt expected her to say yes. Instead, she said: "No, I'm much more likely to worry about a theorem when I'm with my children." (*Science*, October 10, 1979)

~•

One day, the great German mathematician David Hilbert saw a young colleague in tears because his wife had left him. Hilbert put his arm around the young man's shoulder and said comfortingly, "*Es wird convergieren, es wird convergieren!*"—it will converge. What could possibly make a mathematician cry other than an integral that refused to converge?

~•

Dreams seem intense—more gripping—than waking life because they exclude the possibility of reflection. We may think in
a dream, but we can't think about thinking. Does this mean that
animal experience is rather like human dreams?

Fantasy versus imagination. An example of fantasy: when I
say I am Victor Hugo. An example of imagination: when Jean
Cocteau says that Victor Hugo is a madman who thinks he is
Victor Hugo. Alas, most of us are better at fantasy than at being
imaginative.

To apprehend is to risk becoming apprehensive. If we did not
know so much, we would have less to fear. The Stoic philosopher Epictetus said to a fellow passenger, "You are afraid of this
storm as if you were going to have to swallow the whole vast sea;
but, my dear sir, it would take only a quart of water to drown
you." Cardinal Newman asked (in his popular hymn "Lead,
Kindly Light") not to see "the distant scene. One step enough for
me." To see far can cause metaphysical terror, which only God is
able to assuage. "Rock of Ages, cleft for me; / Let me hide myself
in Thee." How desperate this sounds!

Artifacts goad us to evaluate and judge, whether we are
aware of doing so or not. Consider how we respond to a chair
made of wood as distinct from one made of aluminum, a china
cup as distinct from a plastic cup. Things made of natural substances seem restful. We see the wood of the chair and the clay
in the cup, and there thought of a discursive and agitating kind
stops. Not so when we see things made of processed substances,
such as aluminum and plastic. Although we may not know in
any detail the complex technical and economic history of aluminum and plastic, we know that it is there, and this awareness
of human striving—thinking and experimenting—acts as a back-

ground stimulant or irritant that prevents us from feeling totally at ease.

I paint. My landscapes are neither good nor bad: they are just mediocre. Now, suppose I change the title of one of my un-inspired landscapes from *Autumn* to *Mediocrity*, won't the painting suddenly seem good? No longer an unsuccessful attempt at rep-resenting nature, it can now be seen as a highly successful at-tempt at representing mediocrity: every brush stroke speaks of feebleness, of good intention failing to cover up middling talent. A viewer of my work shudders at its cruel realism. How is that for snatching victory from the jaws of defeat?

I also write. Suppose I write an essay titled "Excellence." It fails to persuade, being both logically and stylistically defective. Can I salvage it by changing the title to "Mediocrity"? I suspect not. But why not?

We are told not to be superficial—to look behind appear-ance. How is it that when we look behind beautiful physical phe-nomena (the stars, for example) we find the even greater beauty of physical laws, but when we look behind appealing human phenomena (society, marriage, family) we find only power struggle, class oppression (Marx), and unsavory sex (Freud)?

I feel insecure when I teach away from my home base, and the reason is my near total dependence on my office as I have arranged it over the years: books here, journals there, reprints and notes in filing cabinets to the left of my desk, dictionaries and encyclopedias to the right. I know that all the books in my office can also be found in the library. But that extra effort—the difference between turning to my bookshelf and walking across the street—can kill a burgeoning thought.

My dependence on my office is such that I have come to

think of it as my brain. The brain in my head, by contrast, seems a poor instrument, for no matter how hard I try to pack it with facts and ideas, it always feels empty. And so when I close my office door to go to the classroom, I suffer a moment of panic. What's the good of facing students, all eager to learn, when I have left my brain behind?

"The heat from the sidewalk swims across your shins." This sentence is from a short story, set in California, by John Updike. Technically, there is nothing remarkable about it. I could have written it myself except that I never registered this climatological fact despite my experience of many hot California summers and despite my training as a geographer to notice such things. I know more about temperature gradients than Updike does, but what's the use of such knowledge if my imagination fails to connect it with commonplace human experience?

"If a monkey sits at a typewriter and types at random, the average number of trials before he types perfectly the entire text of Shakespeare's *Hamlet* would be 1 followed by about 40,000 zeroes" (*Science*, vol. 194, 1976). I am fascinated by this fact but don't quite know what conclusion to draw. Would it be that random processes can produce works of the most astonishing order and beauty—snowflakes, for example, and *Hamlet?*

When I disagree with someone, I never say "I disagree." Instead, I say "Yes, but . . . ," which, to my way of thinking, is not only better manners but also more intellectually sound. For a perception or a belief is seldom entirely false. It is false only in the sense that the context in which it is true is too limited, too particular. "The moon is made of cheese," someone says to me. I respond, "Yes, but. Yes, when you are from a cheese-eating culture, yes when the moon that night happens to have the color of cheese, yes when you are tipsy or in a poetic mood. But no, definitely no, when you move out of these and other restricting contexts." In giving my reply this way, I have the support of Blaise Pascal, who wrote: "When we wish to correct with advantage, and to show another that he errs, we must notice from what side he views the matter, for on that side it is usually true, and admit that truth to him, but reveal to him the side on which it is false.... No one is offended at not seeing everything."

Americans like to say "I disagree." That aggressive and uncompromising posture gives one an immediate edge over one's political opponent; and in politics, it is more important to seem right and win than to be tentative and lose. Intellectual discourse, by contrast, requires "Yes, buts..." to move forward at all. Each *yes* confirms a position; each *but* leads to a further refinement or broadening of understanding.

One of my favorite modern plays is John Wesker's *Roots*. In it, the young woman Beatie wants to find her roots and wants her family to help her in her search. When her mother mentions the obvious—her ties with the family farm and its folkways—Beatie explodes in anger and shouts: "God in heaven, Mother, you live in the country but you got no—no—majesty.... Your mind is cluttered up with nothing and you shut out the world. What kind of a life did you give me?" I like the word *majesty*. Searching for roots is supposed to provide one with self-esteem, but what is self-esteem without majesty?

"I understand you." Good.
"I understand you well." Better.
"I understand you completely." Bad—subtly insulting.
And,
"I found you." Good.
"I found you out." Bad.

Necessity is the mother of invention. Or is it leisure, as the distinguished geographer Carl Sauer believes? Actually, both are true: it depends on how one defines *necessity* and *leisure*. Extreme necessity surely beclouds the mind, disabling one from thinking creatively. So the question really is, what degree and kind of necessity may be helpful? Experience suggests the following: an authoritarian political culture combined with room for leisurely private life, as in the former Soviet Union and Soviet-dominated central European countries; well but not extravagantly equipped scientific labs in which the scientists are not beholden to financial backers who might dictate the timing of the results, if not (subtly) the results themselves; genteelly poor graduate students with much vitality and little social responsibility; thinkers and writers of independent (but not ample) means with, often, few familial or social obligations.

In all these examples, leisure is a consequence of necessity — of a lack. The lack is in political-administrative power, money, social weight, and warmth. Historically, some of the world's most creative thinkers suffered from an etiolated social life: they had not reared families or formed close personal ties. Think of Descartes, Newton, Locke, Pascal, Spinoza, Kant, Leibniz, Schopenhauer, Nietzsche, Kierkegaard, and Wittgenstein. (The list is from Anthony Storr's *Solitude*.) In the recent past, talented people in communist countries, lacking political power, had the leisure to direct their energy to areas of imaginative and abstract thought. And then there is the generic young researcher — poor, without the rewards or responsibilities of family life, without much political or administrative power. He or she is operating from necessity — a necessity that, however, opens up time in which to be creative.

The creativity that I have just drawn your attention to is intellectual and literary creativity, which doesn't require much support from society in material resources and labor. But what about large-scale creativity, as, for example, the making of architectural monuments and big science? There, a wealthy and supportive society is obviously necessary. Another example would be movie making, the quintessential art of our time. I am struck by the fact that Chinese movies, whether they are from the mainland or from Taiwan, improved by vast leaps when Chinese society became well-to-do. True, if the word *art* is to be used, we cannot just settle for size and spectacle; human content must also be present. The pleasant surprise there is that spectacle does not exclude subtleties in human relationships. An outstanding example is Ang Lee's *Crouching Tiger, Hidden Dragon,* a movie that has won both critical and popular acclaim.

The naive consumer has time to think. Not, however, the so-called intelligent consumer, who is obliged to read all the fine print on toothpaste tubes and vitamin-pill bottles before making a purchase. The Internet makes serious thinking on important matters even less likely. To ensure the best buy, so much search and research of a time-consuming and technical nature is now necessary that the consumer who succeeds should be awarded a master of science degree.

Consider these extremes. A man using yellow pad and pencil to solve a Fermat theorem. A man using Windows 2000 to solve the problem of making the best buy in a toilet—one that holds enough water to flush properly. O brave new world of consumerism!

Language

I appreciate the following tongue-in-cheek observation made by the linguist Roger Brown in *Words and Things*: "Most people are determined to hold the line against animals. Grant them the ability to make linguistic reference and they will be putting in a claim for minds and souls. The whole phyletic scale will come trooping into Heaven demanding immortality for every tadpole and hippopotamus. Better to be firm now and make it clear that man alone can use language to make reference."

Well, since this was written (the book was published in 1968), chimpanzees and dolphins—if not yet tadpoles and hippo-potami—have made claims to language and some form of sym-bolic thought. The whole phyletic scale *is* pressing hard on our heels, to the distress of human chauvinists and the delight of radical egalitarians. But, whether they are chauvinist or egalitar-ian, the debate is still carried on entirely by human beings. Chimpanzees and dolphins have yet to present their own case. Truly intelligent animals—those from another galaxy, for in-stance—would have reduced human beings to silence rather than stimulate an outpouring of indecisive chatter, as chim-panzees and dolphins do.

Why is it that, in the second half of the twentieth century, we have been so eager to attribute linguistic competence (genuine speech and not just body language) to nonhuman animals? Could it be that with probes into outer space we have finally realized how silent the solar system is—how lonely we are, with only hu-man beings to talk with? As late as the 1940s, it was still possible to envisage "little green men" building canals on Mars. At the time of the publication of C. S. Lewis's science fiction novel *Perelandra* it was still not out of the ballpark to believe that a wise "Green Lady," capable of engaging us in moral debate, lived on the planet Venus. Now, of course, we know better. We are alone. If we want to break out of the human chat room, we have to per-suade ourselves that conversing with chimpanzees and dolphins, to mutual benefit, is plausible.

I wonder whether Brits and Americans are more inclined to attribute language and high intelligence to animals than are Eu-ropeans. Snobbish French Cartesians are perhaps the least likely to be generous. Generally, thinkers influenced by the Enlightenment are stingy. I am struck by the Russian American Vladimir Nabokov's low opinion of our primate cousins. "The gap between ape and man is immeasurably greater than the one between amoeba and ape. The difference between an ape's memory and human memory is the difference between an ampersand and the British Museum library," he wrote in *Strong Opinions*. Even if an American agrees, I doubt he would want to say so in print.

The sharpest difference between a young chimpanzee and a human child is in their ability to sit still and listen. Only a human child truly listens. One of life's deeper pleasures is to read to a four-year-old. There she sits like a little Buddha—her legs crossed, her mouth slightly open—lost in a wonderland of vivid happenings when what reaches her is (from the angle of physical science) only sound waves.

Writing clear expository prose is unnatural, and for this reason I treat it with special respect. In England and France such prose began to appear only in the early part of the seventeenth century. Before then, people favored long, rambling sentences to which clauses were tacked on for no reason other than, possibly, the need to seem as copious and inexhaustible as nature. Poetry deserves less respect because it is almost instinctive to us. Our first sentences are full of poetic turns, as fond parents keep reminding us. The first order of business for those who want to be good writers is to remove fat and adornment—those purple passages that erupt like skin rash—from their prose. Erupt like skin rash. See how easy it is to slip into poetry?

Friends need to be truthful to each other. Yet for the sake of friendship, they also need to show willingness to float above truth. The American novelist David Plante makes this clear with the following story:

I remember when, in my freshman year, I first took Charlie
to visit my parents in our house, remember my worry, as I
opened the door into the entry, that our lives were nowhere
near the level of his family. But Charlie being Charlie, said
to my parents, "What a nice house you have." And, being
me, I said, "Come on, I'll show you around." With each
grim little room I showed him, he said, "This is pretty," and
I'll say, "Isn't it?" We both knew what we were doing, and
knew that this made us friends. With Henry... I would
have had to say, The rooms are grim, and he would have,
of course, agreed. This truthfulness, in a way, precluded
our understanding one another and becoming friends.

How so? Well, I guess the answer is: "This is pretty," followed
by "Isn't it?" are not about architecture and interior decoration
at all; rather they are about mutual fondness. Devious, isn't it,
this human language? No wonder machines have a hard time
learning it.

Wordsworth yearned for a language that all English men and
women could share at the deepest level. For him, this would be
the poetic lyrical language of rural life. Enlightenment figures,
by contrast, preferred the cultivated language of reason, shorn of
emotional excess, for only such a language could transcend local
biases and be widely shared. William Hazlitt (1778–1830) offered a third model—the dramatic model, with its suggestion
of engagement if not confrontation, and the promise of mutual
understanding based on real sympathy, not just polite acquies-
cence. Hazlitt's model, in its highest form, was the Shakespearean drama. In it, kings and beggars, wise men and fools,
men and women, young and old, even though they used different vocabularies and spoke in highly distinctive voices, could
still be communicating members of one great world (the Globe).
Alas, Hazlitt's estimation of Shakespeare's world was too rosy.
He failed to detect that Shakespeare's characters seldom listened.

They addressed not so much one another as the audience. And in addressing and involving the audience—affluent and poor, educated and uneducated, dandies and tradesmen—Shakespeare was surprisingly successful. His technique was to use a very rich language—the richest of any English writer, with Milton a poor second. He indulged in Latinisms, which pleased the learned, but he also spoke street language, which pleased the cobblers and the seamstresses. And he unobtrusively translated Latinisms into plain English. An example from *Twelfth Night:* "But falls into abatement and low price / Even in a minute." *Abatement* is immediately rendered into *low price.* This ability to make the most subtle language understandable must be a reason why the barely educated not only of Shakespeare's time, but also of our own—children, for example—can enjoy Shakespeare.

Shakespeare used a total of 31,534 words in his collected works, 14,376 just once, 4,343 just twice. What a waste! Imagine the effort of learning all those words and then applying them only once or twice in a lifetime. Now, Racine was more efficient. He apparently needed only some 2,000 words to win immortal fame.

Isn't it surprising that, despite the omnipresence and popularity of television, movies, and videos, a record 2.17 billion books were sold in the United States in 1996, up about 20 million copies from the previous year and 100 million from 1993 (*Time*, April 21, 1997)? Well, perhaps it isn't all that surprising when we consider that just about every drugstore, supermarket, and airport sells books and that in bus stations and airports throughout the country it is hard to catch a passenger who doesn't have a paperback in hand, or somewhere in a backpack. The pocket-size book was invented in the sixteenth century, and it has proven to be the most convenient and safest means of escapism known to humankind. With a book, we can be in the Arctic and escape to the tropical forest, in Grand Central Station and escape to Hawaii, in an office rest room and escape to a Bangkok brothel, in the year 2000 and escape to the year 1000. Moreover, the pocket book's flexibility is hard to beat: it can be carried anywhere; we can stop reading at any page, go back to an earlier page or skip to the last one for a glimpse of the ending, or we can read the same passage again and again—the passage that is sexually arousing, for example. The advantage of an obscene passage in a book over the *Playboy* centerfold is that we can savor it in public with an air of innocence, for our neighbor is not likely to know what we are doing by just glancing over our shoulder. Squiggly lines on a page speak to us loud and clear, yet protect our privacy.

What is in a name? John Wisdom was a professor of philosophy at Cambridge. Sir Russell Brain was a distinguished neurophysiologist at Oxford. John Place practiced geography in California. Consider this question: If the name of the surveyor-general of India had been Sir George Higginsbottom rather than Sir George Everest, would the world's tallest mountain be named after him?

What is in a name? T. E. Lawrence (1888–1935) became world famous in the early part of the twentieth century for his quixotic attempt to win independence for the Arabs. Many books were and continue to be written about him. The 1962 movie *Lawrence of Arabia* was well received by critics and a box office triumph. Lawrence himself, however, disdained fame. He sought anonymity by all the means available to him, including that of altering his name legally to T. E. Shaw. But even the name Shaw had too much personality. He wanted to be a mere cipher, which he thought he could be if he joined the Air Force as an ordinary airman. But the big world would not let him alone. Admirers and friends continued to search him out. Playwright Noel Coward sought to reestablish friendship with Lawrence by writing—how? "Dear Shaw" might still sound too familiar. So, what about "Dear 399,40,4286"—Lawrence's registration number? But Coward couldn't resist adding, "May I call you 399?"

I have dined in friends' homes many times, and I know from experience that the food is almost always good. It has obviously been prepared with forethought and skill. A proper sense of values should oblige us to eat in silent appreciation. Yet we chat. What a shame to mix shopworn talk, full of chewed-over clichés, with garden-fresh vegetables and tender sirloin.

One day in Toronto I caught the superintendent of my apartment building swearing at the delivery boy. Out came the words, a hot torrent of abuse. I felt deep sympathy for the hapless boy, but at the same time I couldn't altogether suppress my admiration for the superintendent's Shakespearean fluency. Can I swear as well when the occasion demands it? The answer is no, and I must consider this *no* a yawning gap in my education.

One hundred and sixty years ago, Emerson already regretted the decline of cursing. He wrote on October 24, 1840: "What a pity that we cannot curse and swear in good society! Cannot the stinging dialect of the sailors be domesticated? It is the best rhetoric, and for a hundred occasions those forbidden words are the only good ones."

Is immortality to be won by a mere phrase? Consider "military-industrial complex" (Eisenhower by way of his speechwriter Malcolm Moos) and "crying all the way to the bank" (Liberace). They are now a part of our language. Why do certain phrases catch on and others, though equally eloquent, do not? That Eisenhower and not a sociologist said "military-industrial complex" made the difference. Liberace's contribution can stand on its own merit. Colorful as it is, I still wonder at its wide acceptance. "Finally we die, opposable thumb and all,"

said Herbert Gold. To Nabokov, this sentence is inspired. But it hasn't caught on.

At a conference of landscape architects, I was presented with a plastic pink flamingo—a symbol of bad taste in that profession. I hung it up in my Minneapolis office. People who visited me wondered why. I said, well, I didn't think much of the gift until I remembered that a poet (Robert Penn Warren) saw in the shape of the flamingo's neck "a question" and in its color "passion." Suddenly this piece of cheap garden adornment stood for qualities that I have always admired in a scholar—intellect and passion.

We think that telling a story is something quite different from counting: the one is subjective, the other objective. Both, however, are attempts to give "an account of" reality. (Note that the German word *erzählen*, which means to "relate, tell, report," has at its core *zählen*, which means to "count or compute.")

One mustn't talk shop at a cocktail party. Does this prohibition go back to Louis XIV? He forbade his courtiers to talk about affairs of state during social events, reports W. H. Lewis in *The Splendid Century:* "Even the members of his own family were severely snubbed if they attempted to do so, and it is therefore hardly surprising to find that as early as 1680 the only topic of conversation for the men was hunting and horses, whilst the women talked scandal and frocks."

Not all figures of speech glamorize nature. Here are three put-downs. An outcrop of striated and stained limestone is likened to a pile of dirty laundry. Palm trees are dust mops. Northern lights are shower curtains.

How is it that students don't take more to the study of grammar? As Howard Nemerov has noted, it is full of sexy words: *genitive, dative, conjugate, copula.* Even *active* and *passive* are highly suggestive.

〜

The English language increasingly favors the active voice, a reflection of the power that English speakers increasingly feel they have over events. Thus:

I dreamed. Latin: "It dreamed itself to me."
I remember. Archaic: "It remembers itself to me."

One day, will we say "I occur" rather than "it occurs to me"? Suppose the time comes when we can turn rain on and off at will, will we then say "I rain" rather than "it is raining"?

〜

When the Solzhenitsyns lived in Vermont, Natalie (Aleksandr Isayevich's wife) periodically went back to Moscow for visits. In the subway, she heard the announcement, "Careful! The doors are closing. The next stop is . . ." But it was in Russian! She was home. She felt even more at home when she noticed the words *Moloko* and *Khleb* on a storefront. They immediately conveyed to her something warm and deeply nourishing, in contrast to "Milk" and "Bread," the equivalents she would have encountered in Vermont. Now, Ignat, her son, went to a Vermont school and then to Harvard. When a reporter asked him whether his father ever stopped working, his jazzy reply was: "No, he's never said, 'Today I'm just gonna chill out, take a jog, and blow off this "Red Wheel" [monumental novel] thing'" (*New Yorker,* February 14, 1994). Now, I wonder. What would *Moloko* and *Khleb* mean to Ignat? When his mother used these words, of course he knew what she was referring to. But would this be the same as understanding? Could someone whose natural way of speaking included "gonna chill out" and "blow off this thing" really get into the soul of *Moloko?*

〜

Traditional wisdom has it that one can't be a real scholar and thinker if one can read and think in only one language. But what about those paragons of intellectual virtue, the ancient Greeks? They were essentially monolingual: educated Romans knew Greek, but educated Greeks did not feel the need to know Latin or any other foreign language even when they were curious about non-Greek peoples. (A. Momigliano, "The Fault of the Greeks," *Daedalus*, Spring 1975)

Mist. What a beautiful word in English, calling up, for me, the image of an English meadow early in the morning. But in German it means *crap!* I conclude that anyone with serious poetic ambition can't risk being bilingual.

Michael Borwicz's Ph.D. dissertation, published under the title *Écrits des condamnés à mort sous l'occupation allemand* (Writings of people sentenced to death under the German occupation), used the testimonies of people from all over Europe to communicate their knowledge of what they thought was a radically new reality. Sadly, notes poet Czeslaw Milosz, the words they used were derived from old experience, and so were tired and conventional. Only a true poet could have done justice to the unprecedented horror of death in a concentration camp, but he could have done so only by distancing himself from the numbing reality and immersing himself in a linguistic wonderland of choice words and syntax. Isn't there something morally ambiguous in such an undertaking? Paradoxically, the dull conventional words—in their desperate inadequacy—could seem more honest and telling.

Morality

"What is truth?" Pilate asked. One who ought to know chose silence as his answer. Hannah Arendt noted that none of the higher religions except Zoroastrianism included lying among the sins. There is no simple commandment: Thou shalt not lie.

For Goethe, propriety is a criterion of truth. Or, to put it another way, truth resides in a balanced vision in which religious, aesthetic, and moral perceptions are at one. Nietzsche admired Goethe for this view of truth, which he described as characteristic of the aristocratic mind; and to Nietzsche, Goethe was the last of the great aristocratic minds. Since then, a plebeian turn has taken over: truth is now coupled with itching curiosity, the desire to dive in an orgy of self-abasement into the darkest recesses of the human body and soul, a certain psychological tactlessness, and "a sniggering suspicion of the absence of meaning in anything that evades definition or experimental proof, and above all a disregard for those intangible qualities that make the world a noble habitation" (Eric Heller, *The Importance of Nietzsche*).

"We are all capable of evil thoughts, but only very rarely of evil deeds; we can all do good deeds, but very few of us can think good thoughts." This is the remark of the Italian author Cesare Pavese. Yet he himself contradicted it, for he committed suicide in 1950 (an evil deed), shortly after he received Italy's highest literary award, the Strega Prize.

Kindness is winning over love—alas—in our increasingly secular age. Kindness seeks happiness for its object. Love, by contrast, seeks the beloved's rise to the heights of his or her being. Kindness is unambiguously appropriate to animals. We should want them to be happy—that is, well fed, well housed, and healthy. We should want happiness for human beings too. But not unconditionally. An important difference between kindness and love is that love is far more demanding. It realizes that for the beloved to attain true dignity and fulfillment, joy rather than mere happiness, he or she may have to postpone satisfaction (happiness) and embrace a discipline that can be frustrating and painful.

Kindness implies an asymmetrical relationship: one is kind toward the needy and the weak. It is hard to be kind and not also somewhat condescending. Love, by contrast, is far more an affair between equals. God himself, infinitely above us, yet makes himself our "equal," by seeming to need our love.

Kindness is ultimately indifferent to its object. It does what it can for the stray cat or for the abused woman, and then they are forgotten. Love is never indifferent, even when it pushes the beloved—a child, for example—away, so that she can be independent, free to live a life and build a world of her own.

Kindness, which demands far less time and energy than love, can be applied to many more individuals. That's one big advantage it has over love. We ought to practice kindness whenever and wherever opportunities arise, if only because it is within our moral reach, yet never forget that it is weak tea compared with love.

John Henry Cardinal Newman (1801–90) defined the gentleman as "one who never inflicts pain . . . his great concern being to make everyone at their ease and at home." Well, I hope Cardinal Newman was no gentleman, for his religion taught that mere kindness would not have been enough to get him into heaven. Cardinal Newman had to love, and that might mean an occasional honesty that could cause pain. On the other hand, how easy it is for people to masquerade their indifference and cruelty under the label of "tough love."

Philo of Alexandria (20 B.C.–A.D. 50): "Be kind, for everyone you meet is fighting a great battle."

In a universe in which time reversal is possible, as some physicists think, effect can precede cause, and the human conception of justice goes out of the window, as the White Queen in *Through the Looking-Glass* foretold:

WHITE QUEEN: "The King's Messenger is in prison now; the trial doesn't even begin until next Wednesday; and of course the crime comes last of all."
ALICE: "Suppose he never commits the crime?"
WHITE QUEEN: "That would be all the better, wouldn't it?"

In 1999 Dr. Wen-ho Lee, a Chinese American scientist at Los Alamos National Laboratory, was put in jail and shackled for the crime of having passed nuclear-bomb secrets affecting national security to a hostile nation. What about a trial? Oh, that would come later—much later. What about the crime? What if that particular crime was never committed? Responded the White Queen (Attorney General Janet Reno): "That would be all the better, wouldn't it?"

Justice presupposes the existence of law, to which one can appeal when one feels that an injustice has been done. What about fairness? "That's not fair!" we say bitterly, to which the wise and sad response can only be, "But life (or God) is not fair."

A Russian tale has it that God comes to a peasant one day and offers to grant him any wish in the world. The peasant is excited and starts fantasizing about what he can have. "Just remember," God says, "whatever you choose, I will do twice as much for your neighbor as I do for you." The peasant is stumped because he cannot bear to think of his neighbor being so much better off. Finally, he comes up with a bright idea and tells God: "Strike out one of my eyes and take out both eyes of my neighbor."

Well, if God asked me, I would put on my best Sunday face and say, "Please, give me generosity." God would have to commend me for requesting a virtue rather than material wealth. But, of course, if I am made generous, my neighbor will be made doubly generous, which means that every time I give him some-thing, he will have to give me twice the amount in return. Moral: bourgeois cunning and calculation go further than peas-ant jealousy and resentment.

Jealousy and resentment are, in one respect, more destructive than hatred. Hatred is surgical: one can destroy one's enemy without destroying oneself. Jealousy and resentment, by con-trast, splash destruction all around. A weakness in democracy is its tendency to encourage resentment, says Alexis de Toc-queville. "I am as good as you are" may be good affirmation at the level of egalitarian politics, but it has the pernicious effect of disabling oneself from admiring excellence in another, which amounts to an inability to enjoy life.

We owe our parents love and respect because they have given us birth and have nurtured us. Some such belief is probably uni-versal. Gratitude to parents for nurturing us is easy to under-stand. More problematic is gratitude for giving us birth. In the old days, I imagine a child reasoning as follows: "My parents didn't exactly plan my birth. It was the sort of thing that hap-pened after marriage. In a sense, Mother Nature gave me birth, my parents being the instruments. If I must show gratitude, it would be to Mother Nature." In our time, the child will have to reason differently. She will say, "Well, my mother could have aborted me if she so chose, for it would have been her right. But she didn't. Like a goddess, she graciously permitted me to exist. For this, I owe her gratitude. On the other hand, I also feel di-minished. Is my existence, which seems to me of the utmost importance, merely the result of a choice that could have gone the other way? My sense of diminishment is compensated, how-ever, by the thought that, one day, I too will have the right to make up my mind as to whether another will live."

A life is human if, *whatever its present state,* it can in time and
without resorting to heroic means become an individual capable
of enjoying the world in roughly the same way that other human
beings do. Other definitions are possible, of course, but will they
be as economical and will they as effectively prevent us from
terminating a life on the grounds that it cannot survive without
the almost constant care of a person or society? (Remember that
this "it" can be a comatose patient or a mentally retarded person,
as well as a fetus or an infant.) In any fair deliberation, no doubt
the well-being of the caring agent must also be considered, and
there is no gainsaying that the fetus is a burdensome parasite on
its mother. But so is the newborn infant! Indeed, the infant is
worse: for one thing, it bawls tyrannically, as the fetus never
does. Why, then, the extraordinary difference in the way they
are treated? The ancient Romans seem to me more logical.
Roman parents were ardently prochoice: they would be furious
if they were denied the right to decide whether their babies
should live or die.

Almost all arguments against abortion rest on the belief that
the unborn is already human. The evidence is usually drawn from
science. But it can also be drawn from famous legends. Here is
one from the Bible, as told by Mother Teresa in *No Greater Love:*
"As soon as Mary received the announcement from the angel, she
went in haste to her cousin Elizabeth, who was with child. And
the unborn child, John the Baptist, rejoiced in Elizabeth's womb."
Mother Teresa added: "How wonderful it was—Almighty God
chose an unborn child to announce the coming of His Son!"

"We hold these truths to be self-evident, that all men are
created equal." The Founding Fathers meant "all *English*men and
property owners are created equal," but as good rhetoricians
they knew that the power of that declaration would be emascu-
lated if they had added the qualifiers. Ever since, American conscience has been haunted by the rhetoric, which goes to show

that rhetoric, even though it may sound at first empty and hypocritical, has consequence. Moral progress is a matter of making hypocrisy pay—sooner or later.

Diseases spread, but not health. Who has heard of an epidemic of health? Malicious rumor spreads, but not generous praise. Given evil's motility, far surpassing (it would seem) good's, it's a wonder that the world is as good as it is.

Our moral terms are permeated by the values of a bygone feudal age, as Mary McCarthy reminds us in *Birds of America:* "Villain and clown are just words for peasant. Rogue is the worst thing Hamlet could think of calling himself, and yet it means simply beggar." *Low, base, mean, boorish* are all synonyms for *vulgar* (that is, characteristic of the common people), whereas *noble, gentle, and kind* (and even such middle-class-sounding terms as *free* and *frank*) mean the aristocratic.

Winston Churchill liked to claim that he was a descendant of a Seneca Indian, as though being a descendant of the duke of Marlborough was not enough. Surely the most widely accepted image of nobility today is that of an Indian brave in profile. How come? The answer is that the Indian stands for the warrior virtue of courage: in the mythic imagination, Indians were killed, never slaughtered. By contrast, the Chinese never projected an image of nobility to foreigners—or even to themselves. Churchill would never have claimed Chinese blood, even if it was mandarin.

Fashion spreads downward, from the elite to the people. However, it can also go the other way. I am reminded of this each time I walk by Urban Outfitters, a shop for upscale undergraduates, and see in the display windows artfully arranged clothes that look as though they have been picked up from a Goodwill bin. (The year was 1987.) City planners do not yet favor the slum as a planning ideal. But who knows? Already, avant-garde photographers may select a paper-strewn parking lot or a wall covered in graffiti as a chic background for high fashion. As for morals, their trajectory has also been reversed. Manners once favored by the upper class that took them centuries to refine—gentleness, soft-spokenness, understatement— have gone the way of sartorial restraint and elegance. In today's driven world, they are considered wussy. It is true that frankness and freedom, once also aristocratic exclusives, have managed to retain their value as they percolated down the layers of society, but among the fervent well-to-do young of our time, this is true only if frankness rises to aggression and freedom rises to anarchy and violence.

Who says we haven't made moral progress? Just look at the decline of sexism and ageism in the twentieth century. When the *Titanic* sank on April 14, 1912, more than 80 percent of those who drowned were men. Many had relinquished their lifeboat seat to women. In a recent survey, only 35 percent of the men on *Titanic II* would today cede their lifeboat seat to children or to women who weren't their wives. (*Time*, April 27, 1992)

It is often said that we kill people with ease because we consider them subhuman. Yet GIs affectionately called German soldiers "Fritz" or "Jerry" during the Second World War, and called Viet Cong guerrillas "Charlie" during the Vietnam War. How come?

I weigh the equivalent of 17,697,000 insects. Because I assume in clear conscience that my life is worth more than those

of arthropods, I would not hesitate to favor mine when a choice
has to be made. But where do I draw line? At what point on the
scale of numbers will I—should I—begin to have qualms?

Lunds, an upscale supermarket in Minneapolis, once advised
its customers not to hesitate to plunge live lobsters into boiling
water. Sure, they might feel some pain, but then they were—so
Lunds claimed—monsters of iniquity in their own world.

A *New Yorker* cartoon, some years back, shows lobsters tucking
in their napkins as they prepare to dine on humans in a fancy
restaurant. You can see naked humans swimming in a water tank,
all with their hands tied behind their back. I don't know why,
but what bothers me most—whether it is the lobsters or the
humans—is that their claws or hands are tied. That, to me,
stands for ultimate powerlessness and humiliation.

Herman Melville to his hypocrite reader: "Go to the meat-
market of a Saturday night and see the crowds of live bipeds
staring up at the long rows of dead quadrupeds. . . . Cannibals?
Who is not a cannibal?"

After listening to a recording of Bach's Cello Sonata no. 6,
I felt good. I even felt that I had become a better human being.
I went to the post office. There was a long line. As the customers
ahead of me shuffled forward with maddening slowness and un-
predictability, I found myself wishing—to my horror—for their
liquidation! Nothing messy, mind you, just their nonexistence,
so that I—*I!*—could be served.

At the airline ticket counter, inevitably someone holds up the
line with some persnickety request—vegetarian food, but no

bean sprouts, please. Even as I wish for the nonexistence of those ahead of me, I can feel hostile eyes drilling into my back, for no doubt those behind me see *me* as the nuisance best kicked aside. If the circle around the campfire is a good image of heaven, the waiting line at the busy airport—in itself a display of order and courtesy—is, for me, a good image of hell.

How does a welfare mother feel waiting to see a haughty bureaucrat? Waiting, for her, is a fixture of life, not just an occasional nuisance. I excoriate my impatience—the presumption that my time (life) is so valuable that none can be wasted. Waiting, I say to myself, is good for my soul. But to no avail. Why waste breath preaching morality to others when, directed at myself with all the logic at my command, it does no good at all?

There ought to be some sort of balance between the quality of one's material environment and the quality of one's moral life. Living in a bad place, one can be excused for being bad oneself, but as the environment improves so ought one's moral life. I use "ought" in two senses: that of environmental influence, the belief that a place has impact; and that of obligation, the belief that, with hot and cold running water and even air-conditioning, one is obliged to upgrade one's behavior to match—or suffer the neurosis of disjunction. All this explains why I have not sought to improve my material environment in the past fifteen years. I don't want to put a long-held geographical hypothesis (environmental influence) to the test. More importantly, I don't want the stress of being a better person than I am.

In this, I am influenced by Albert Schweitzer's notion of a secret tax that we ought to impose on ourselves when we allow ourselves goods that go beyond the essential. He writes in *A Place for Revelation: Sermons on Reverence for Life*: "If you undertake a vacation trip, then set aside a gift that will go to the poor and the sick to get them out of the muggy city air. If you make a celebration for your relatives or friends, then ration your means so that you can offer the hungry the same amount you enjoyed to help them. If you buy a piece of furniture or something else that gives you pleasure, think about granting something in the same value for those who lack the most necessary things."

Well, you see how it is. Like all rich people, I try to avoid paying tax—in this case, the secret tax that conscience imposes. However, I make an exception of buying books, which I have well beyond the number I strictly need. My rationalization in regard to books is that in teaching, writing, and perhaps even conversation I do return to the world something of what I have acquired. That "something" is the tax. Still, how little it is compared to my income.

My appearance, mental ability, and disposition, my vitality—so much of me is determined by the genetic code I was born with. "I can accept that," as young Americans say when harsh facts leave them no wiggle room. I can accept that and a lot of other things too, but what I find least acceptable is the lack in me of a *natural* disposition to be good, for I have come to believe that being good is a talent like any other. Of course, one can will to be good, learn to be good, but such efforts have their limitations, and can even be counterproductive, making one into a prig or moral fundamentalist rather than one who effortlessly hits the right moral note on every occasion.

I am ambivalent about the memorial service, which, as every freshman anthropologist knows, is conducted for the benefit of the living. Memorializing the dead makes us feel good about ourselves. It encourages us to neglect friends while they are still alive in the belief that it is never too late to make up. Worse, it allows us to be sentimental—to pour out feelings that run no risk of being cashed.

Albert Schweitzer and Jean-Paul Sartre were kinsmen. It is clear that they had little sympathy for each other's outlooks. Schweitzer took offense at something Sartre wrote in his auto-

biography, *The Words*, and retaliated with the following observation: "I met Sartre very early, when he was still in his baby
clothes. I lived near my uncle, close to the Bois de Boulogne and
so my cousin often asked me to push the pram to the park for
her. I was supposed to lift him out of the pram to do a wee-wee;
but he never did it when he was lifted out, only in the pram.
One could see that he was already himself in that pram."

How sad to see this unseemly tiff between two moral and intellectual giants of the twentieth century. And sad, too, that I
should bring it to your attention.

When E. M. Forster was seventy-seven years old and had
just been awarded the Order of Merit by the queen, he said to
a friend that he had "often the feeling of wanting to steal, and
thinking how clever it would be of [him]." It is not the desire to
steal, but confessing the feeling of how clever it would be to do
so, just after his initiation into the inner sanctum of the Establishment, that is the true Forster touch.

Looking back on her childhood, Dorothy Day of the
Catholic Worker Movement thought of those years as a happy
time and expressed gratitude to her parents for the quietness and
security of her life: "To draw the curtains at night on a street
where people bent against the wind, and where a steady whirl
of snowflakes blurred the outlines of trees, and to turn to a room
where a fire glowed, this was comfort, security, peace, community." Thus, even to a saint (Day was a saint to the down-and-
outs and to poet W. H. Auden and other New York intellectuals),
the cozy comfort of one's own world depends on seeing people
outside it "bent against the wind."

Children boast of their accomplishments to parents; likewise,
pupils to teachers. When they do, they know that they will win
approval *and* give pleasure. The same happens when a husband

boasts to his wife, according to John Maynard Keynes. He thought that many men married just to have a wife to boast to. At the time, Keynes was single. And though he had many friends and liked to show off, he couldn't because it would arouse a displeasure that was all the more gangrenous because it couldn't be vented. The single person is lonely for many reasons, one of which is the lack of opportunity to brag and please at the same time.

Fame, that "last infirmity of noble mind" (Milton). Joseph Conrad, toward the end of his life, yearned for the Nobel Prize. So, apparently, did Robert Frost, James Thurber, and W. H. Auden—all immortals even without that Swedish accolade. If only human beings were more proud than vain! Pride is a power-ful antidote to vanity. Of course, humility is a better antidote, but it isn't as easy to acquire.

In his book *Arabian Sands*, Wilfrid Thesiger tells several stories of the extraordinary generosity of extremely poor Bedouins. Here is one. It concerns his companion, Bin Kabina, a boy who, though almost destitute himself, gives away first his loincloth, and then his shirt, to someone he thought was even worse off.

"God, why did you do that when you have only a rag to wear?"

"He asked me for it."

"Damn the man. I gave him a handsome present. Really you are a fool."

"Would you have me refuse him when he asked for it?"

Since Napoleon's invasion and occupation of Egypt (1798–1801), Europeans have been fascinated by the dry swath that spans North Africa and the Middle East. The antiquities— above all, the pyramids—were a source of fascination, but the barrenness of the desert itself exercised a certain magic. For some reason, English men and women were particularly partial to a landscape that in many ways was the opposite of the cozy green hills and dales of their native country. Charles Doughty, Gertrude Bell, Norman Douglas, T. E. Lawrence, Freya Stark, and Thesiger himself are some of the famous names with a literary reputation. Without doubt, the most famous of all is T. E. Lawrence, or Lawrence of Arabia. He created an image of the desert that is in many ways antilife; and I think the same antilife image can be discerned in the writings of the other desert travelers. The stress is on mineral sterility, but a sterility that is also purity, a sterility that, moreover, paradoxically highlights the preciousness and beauty of the life that does exist—oases dwarfed by vast expanses of sand and rock, flowers that come to ephemeral bloom after a rare rain shower, the lone human figure riding on the back of a camel. Life in the desert attains a dignity that it loses in the rain forest. The rarity of life is a source of its dignity, but as important is its transience. The blooming flower does not last; nothing—other than stone—lasts. A human life certainly doesn't. So why strive to sustain it? Why this constant ignoble urge to survive? Why not give away one's food and clothes—one's life—if such a gesture temporarily helps another?

Now, there is a dark side—anti-Semitism—in the values I just articulated. English intellectuals adored the Arabs for the simplicity, sparseness, and freedom of their lives. Nothing much can accumulate in the desert. By contrast, in the great European commercial cities, what else is there but ceaseless, greedy accumulation? Ironically, even this bias in favor of sparsity, against plenitude, in favor of the desert, against the Land of Milk and Honey, owes its origin to Jewish belief. For it is in the Old Testament, particularly in the pronouncement of the pre-exilic prophets, that one finds the earliest and most eloquent articulation of the nomadic-pastoral or desert ideal. Where does one find God? Where does God speak directly to his people? Why, in the desert, not in the villages and towns of Canaan—places tempted by mammon worship and godless wealth. (See John W. Flight, "The Nomadic Idea and Ideal in the Old Testament," *Journal of Biblical Literature*, vol. 42, 1923.)

◦∵

Generosity is a quality C. S. Lewis had in abundance, and it shows in his literary criticism. *Criticism* may not even be the right word, for he chooses not to waste time attacking, preferring instead to praise with the aim of rescuing excellences that may otherwise be overlooked. However, his generosity can be excessive, according to A. N. Wilson, and so mislead the reader. An example is Lewis's expounding of Lydgate's *The Fall of Princes*. He quotes the lovely lines—"And as I stoode myself alloone upon the Nuwe Yeare night, / I prayed unto the frosty moone, with her pale light"—not telling the reader that the bulk of the book is dull almost beyond bearing.

John Bayley says of Iris Murdoch that he "never met anyone less naturally critical or censorious." Yet Murdoch was a notable philosopher and novelist. One can, of course, attack a person's ideas without making it into an attack on the person. Someone like Murdoch can therefore be a philosopher. But a novelist? Is this why I find Murdoch's bad characters rather overdrawn—thin and melodramatic? Good philosophers can be saintly—Socrates, G. E. Moore, and Wittgenstein come to mind—but I find it hard to see how they could also be good novelists.

William James was another one of those human beings too generous by nature to be a good critic. His biographer John Jay Chapman wrote: "He seemed to me to have too high an opinion of everything. The last book he had read was always 'a great book'; the last person he had talked with, a wonderful being."

Charles Darwin was a bit like that too. In contrast to clever friends like Thomas Huxley, whose instinct upon seeing a new book was to attack—to break (as it were) its spine—Darwin's first reading of almost any book was sympathetic. His critical intellect became seriously engaged only during a second reading. This way, Darwin argued, he could benefit from even second-rate books.

Don't forget Homer, the father of Western literature. His works glow because, however grimly and realistically they may portray life on the battlefield, their overall effect is one of wholesomeness that comes, ultimately, from a love of—and a generosity toward—the world. As the rhetor Dio of Prusa put it: "Homer praised almost everything—animals and plants, water and earth, weapons and horses. He passed over nothing without somehow honoring and glorifying it. Even the one man whom he abused, Thersites, he called a clear-voiced speaker."

I wonder whether there is any great work of literature—a work that is treasured and read over the centuries—that is not also, at bottom, a song of praise.

Ironically, clever worldly writers are not worldly enough. If they really want to remain in the world longer than a season, they must be more wholesome, show more delight with "animals and plants, water and earth, weapons and horses," be more like Homer and Tolstoy, William James and Charles Darwin, and, at another level, C. S. Lewis and Iris Murdoch.

Devotion to truth can make one effortlessly generous. So it seemed with Bertrand Russell. Devastated by Wittgenstein's criticism of his work, Russell nevertheless could rejoice when he heard that Wittgenstein's work was going well. He wrote to Lady Ottoline Morrell: "You can hardly believe what a load this lifts off my spirits—it makes me feel almost young and gay."

At the University of Wisconsin at Madison, I developed a special fondness for Russian exchange students (Valentin Bogorov, Dmitri Sidorov, and Denis Vizgalov) and for visiting professor L. Serebryanny. What do I find in them? Space, which is my shorthand for largeness of spirit. And depth, by which I mean the Russian soul, an intuitive understanding of suffering, or just unhappiness, in another. What about Americans? Of course, I am fond of them too. And again I find myself reverting to the figure of space, which speaks to me of generosity and the dreaming of wild dreams. As for depth, well, one does not speak of the American soul as one does the Slavic (or Russian) soul. Americans have not suffered enough. African Americans are the exception. They have suffered on the Slavic scale, and, interestingly, they are the only Americans who have soul and feel free to talk about it.

In a world whose moral language is cluttered with entitlements and rights, there is less and less room for gratitude—for the likes of Teresa of Avila, who said that she could be bought with a sardine, so easily overcome was she by any gesture of kindness.

Uncommon is not so much the feeling of gratitude as open expression of it. Jesus cured ten lepers, but only one bothered to return to thank him. Jesus himself seemed surprised. "Where are the nine?" he asked (Luke 17:12–18). Jorge Luis Borges asked the publisher of his first book, "How many copies have you sold?" The publisher's despondent reply, 127 copies. Borges was jubilant. "So many people bought my book when they had thousands to choose from!" He was so grateful that he wanted to have the addresses of all the buyers so that he could send each a personal letter of thanks.

Dorothy Day separated from her lover after years of living together and the birth of a child. They couldn't come to an agreement on thankfulness. When Dorothy Day fell in love with Forster and he with her, she felt a pressing need to thank someone, and told him so. She took for granted that he would understand, for mutual understanding was one of the forces that held them together. Yet, in this instance, Forster failed to grasp her need. While he was grateful to hear of her affection and gratitude, he just couldn't see why there had to be someone to thank.

Middle-school student Michael Carter was constantly fidgeting with his baggy pants, to the annoyance of his teacher Jane Smith, who asked him to stop. He replied that he couldn't help fidgeting, that he suffered from a kidney disease, was on dialysis and in need of a kidney transplant. Ms. Smith said: "Well, I have two. Do you want one?" The story of the transplant quickly caught the country's attention, in part because Michael is black and Ms. Smith white, reported the *New York Times* (December 18, 1999). Ms. Smith couldn't understand what all the fuss in the media was about. It seemed to her the natural thing to do. Michael's mother was overwhelmed with gratitude. She thanked the Lord for "that lady," for "Jane Smith." She said she was getting bold, even tough, with the Lord: "Don't you ever let her want for anything, Lord. Don't even let her want for a Kleenex." She explained: "I mean, I was going down the list, because I couldn't ever repay her enough for what she had done."

"I ask Thee not my joys to multiply, / Only to make me worthier of the least," wrote Elizabeth Barrett Browning.

When something bad happens to us, we feel not only miserable but also offended, as though an injustice has been done. When something good happens to us, do we ever say, "Wait a minute, that's unearned"?

"The business of a wise man is to be happy," opined Dr. Johnson. He showed a distaste for what he called the "hypocrisy of misery" and the "affectation of distress" in his fellow human beings. Happiness can seem at times almost a moral quality. Is this why we consider children good? They are often genuinely happy—real suckers for God's and human creations.

I am in favor of animals' rights, but I would go a step further and argue for animals' obligations, without which animal dignity will always be somewhat impaired. Why, after all, should noblesse oblige be restricted to human beings? Isn't it just conceivable that the grizzly bear, newly endowed with rights, would feel obligated to help old ladies across the street?

Of Frederick Mosteller, distinguished statistician and former president of the American Association for the Advancement of Science, William Kruskal wrote: "He will demand more of himself than of others." Well, I pay others the compliment of demanding more of *them*. It's one of my few admirable traits.

"Christ tells us to aim very high, not to be like Abraham or David or any of the saints, but to be like our heavenly Father," Mother Teresa said. Having no less a personage than God for a role model is all very well, but won't such high aiming lead to elitism? Saints are elitists by nature—that is to say, they want everyone, without exception, to show themselves as indeed the crème de la crème of creation, ranking only a little below the angels. Mother Teresa, in her high estimation of human possibility, is merely echoing another saint, Heinrich Suso (1295–1366), who wrote: "God has not called his servants to a mediocre, ordinary life, but rather to the perfection of a sublime holiness, since he said to his disciples: 'Be ye perfect as your heavenly Father is perfect.'"

One starving person makes me sad. Two make me sadder. Three make me sadder still, and so on. In the thought and feeling of a spectator, the *sum* of human suffering means something. But what can the sum mean to the individual sufferers? Will one person's hunger pangs increase when he knows that other hungry people live in the neighborhood? If my tooth aches more because I know that yours aches, too, I won't want your company. Hospitals will be screaming hells. Contemporary thinkers who have considered this question and came to the same conclusion as the one I have just noted include George Bernard Shaw, C. S. Lewis, Ludwig Wittgenstein, and Jorge Luis Borges. They are very different people, yet in this area of moral psychology they appear to think alike. Are they right? If so, does "the *sum* of suffering" become meaningless?

Beauty is a signpost beckoning us to rise to philosophical and spiritual heights. So say the ancient Greeks. It works for me: our lovely university campus and its "limpid, liquid youths" (Gerard Manley Hopkins) propel me effortlessly to higher thoughts. But what if one aspires to moral excellence? Then, not beauty but ugliness is the only reliable signpost. For ugliness is a reminder of death, and unless one is able to face death, or ugliness—its chilly foreshadowing—one cannot hope to be strong morally, a good person. There is plenty of physical deformity on the University of Wisconsin campus, more or less concentrated in the Memorial Union, where, besides students, the old and the lonely, the mentally retarded and the paraplegic congregate. As I sit in the Lakefront Cafe, looking at a retarded person throwing temper tantrums and slopping food all over himself, I see my own future in a nursing home. Rather than learn compassion, I learn fear.

Social injustice is bad, but it can be fixed. I am less sanguine about biological injustice. Consider ugliness—a biological misfortune that severely impairs one's quality of life. In a famous example from literature, Frankenstein's monster yearns for acceptance—for friendship. "But that cannot be; the human senses are insurmountable barriers to [his] union" with other people. In decency, we try not to feel repulsed. But it is not easy, for our visual sense latches onto surface appearance and judges it with instinctive finality.

Then there is beauty. Think how pleasant it is to know, not in any self-conscious or offensive way, that by simply walking into a room one makes a contribution, brightening its atmosphere and the mood of the people in it.

What if the creature made in some human laboratory is not a monster but a cute, loving boy called David? Steven Spielberg poses that question in his movie *A.I.: Artificial Intelligence* without offering any clear answer. The human couple who adopt David as a substitute for their real son, Martin, comatose in a hospital and unlikely to recover, are at first much taken by David, but they reject him (it?) when Martin miraculously recovers and returns home. To moviegoers, David is undoubtedly the more appealing of the two boys. However, David's appeal is subtly undermined by the moviegoers' awareness that he is programmed to be good—that he can neither think nor do evil, as Martin can, because he has no free will. Spielberg's fantasy raises the old theological question, Why didn't God create only Davids? Wouldn't the world be more beautiful, and everyone in it happier? Yes, maybe. But in such a world, there will be no room for the movie *A.I.: Artificial Intelligence*, which I, for one, much enjoyed.

We can't help being influential, for good or ill. That's why life is stressful to a conscientious person. True, a big rock makes a bigger splash than a little one, but the waves generated in either case sooner or later reach the farthest shore.

Our twisted psychology is at the root of so much evil. What do I mean by twisted psychology? I mean this. Whereas past injuries and humiliations lurk in our memory, ready to emerge in full force at the least provocation, the kindnesses and favors that have come our way all too quickly fade. They fade because we take them to be ours by right. Suppose it were otherwise. Suppose it is not injury but good that lurks in our memory, ever ready to pounce? Won't we feel so much more alive, our days filled with wonder and gratitude?

Religion

It is hard to tell a good Christmas story when Christianity has lost its mythic power and become just secular good works and mindless moral crusading. But I do have such a story. Some forty years ago, when I taught at Indiana University, I attended a social sciences conference in Lexington, Kentucky. The morning sessions were crushingly dull. I decided to skip the afternoon ones and go home. By the time I drove into Indiana, darkness blotted out much of the landscape and snow was beginning to fall. I checked into a hotel in a small border town whose name I can no longer remember. Its Main Street was strewn with Christmas decorations, but few shoppers were around. The town looked abandoned. In my hotel room I turned off the lights, slumped on the bed, and fell into deep sleep. I woke up not knowing where I was. Ah, yes, Indiana. I stared at a patch of red light on the ceiling that flicked on and off—reflections from a neon sign outside. Rather than risk drifting off to sleep again, I forced myself to get up and go out. The cold air felt good. I trudged the snow-covered streets to find something to eat. Only one café was open. I went in and sat in a booth by the window. The menu killed my appetite. I asked the waitress for coffee and a doughnut. While she was gone, I peered out of the window. How dark the street had become. "Wait a minute!" I said to myself, "What has happened to all the Christmas lights and decorations?" I turned around to check the room. No sign of Christmas there either—no greeting cards, plastic Santas, or aluminum-foil stars. No cardboard manger. How could this be? Why was the glitz removed, and how could it be done so quickly?

The waitress returned with my order. To my queries, which grew more and more frenzied, she showed, first, puzzlement, then alarm. "Look," she said, "drink this coffee and eat the doughnut and you will feel better."

The point of my story is not that the world has gone secular, that people no longer embrace the Christian faith; rather that there *never was such a faith*. My shock lay in catching a glimpse of a world that never had known the Sermon on the Mount, Chartres cathedral, Michelangelo's *Pièta*, Bach's *Matthew Passion*, and Handel's "Hallelujah Chorus," a world minus the religion—the ethos and inspiration—that made these works possible.

Holy Communion, the central rite of Christianity, has eating at its core. What holds people together in Communion is not a belief or doctrine, which necessarily varies with an individual's background and education, but rather the simple, universal act of taking food. Eating in itself is self-serving. Yet when people eat together, a self-serving private act becomes profoundly communal—a communion. Or rather it can be that. Some reaching out of awareness and sympathy is necessary. Here I am, my hunger assuaged by food that others have prepared; here I am, content and grateful. A brother, neighbor, or total stranger sitting next to me is having the same basic experience. Knowing how another feels—knowing in the depth of my being that that feeling is reciprocated and heightened by reciprocation—is communion. The upwelling of gratitude is worship. Note that the food at the table is bread and wine, universal in intent if not in fact; it cannot be a regional specialty.

"Take no thought what ye shall eat or what ye shall drink, or wherewithal ye shall be clothed. For after all these things do the Gentiles seek. But seek first the kingdom of God and His righteousness, and all these things shall be added unto you" (Matthew 6:31–33). Well, in our secular age, we spend an inordinate amount of time thinking about what we eat and drink. Diet is our guiding angel, health our holy grail. Contrary to Jesus, we say, "Seek first a good diet, and the kingdom of God—that is to say,

health, happiness, and good communal relationships—will be
added unto you."

Historically, sacred places were places of thunder and lightning—places of power and awe. Morality did not enter the picture until the Jews, for the first time in human history, identified
the numinous Presence on dark mountaintops with "the *righteous*
Lord" who "loveth righteousness" (Psalms, 11:7). Again, it was
the great Jewish prophets who belittled the mere mechanisms of
sacrifice and, by implication, sacred places by declaring that, ultimately, the only action totally pleasing to God was justice. And
it remains so today. But what is justice? Obviously, it cannot be
treating oneself and one's own kind well, and it cannot be remembering past injustices done to oneself. What is it then? The
great Jewish prophets would have answered: treat *others*—
strangers beyond the gate—fairly and compassionately; and in
the year 2001, they can only be the homeless and impoverished
Palestinians.

Places have power. Sacred groves and mountaintops have
awesome power such that if you approach them without ritual
purification you risk death, just as, nowadays, if you enter a nu-
clear plant without purification—symbolized by the putting on
of a white protective suit—you risk death. But, as I have just
said, a different notion of power came into being with the Jews.
Henceforth, power manifests itself as peace and justice, not as
lightning and thunder, turbulence and violence. This means that
if you enter a sacred place, you risk not death but Life. In other
words, you risk becoming a holy (that is, wholesome) person, a
more just and compassionate person. Pray at the Western Wall
and you will end up feeling an irresistible urge to embrace a
Palestinian neighbor, such is the wall's sacred power.

What I have said about the Jews applies equally to the Arabs.
After all, Islam is an offshoot of the older religions of Christianity and Judaism. Allah is power, but power for good; Allah cannot help being good—it is his nature. Enter his holy place and
you will become, willy-nilly, a better person. And so the Arabs

who have just prayed at the Al-Aqsa Mosque will emerge from it feeling an irresistible urge to embrace their Jewish neighbors.

What if none of the above is true? What if, after praying at the wall and in the mosque, Jews and Arabs both feel more self-righteous and resentful, each more ready to condemn the other, more willing to fight the other? Doesn't this imply that neither the wall nor the mosque can be a genuine sacred place? For both are demonstrably without power—unless, shockingly, their power is the power to incite hatred and conflict.

Jerusalem is a holy city. But can it be holy if it generates so much hatred? The streets and squares, the very air, seem to promote conflict. By contrast, there is Madison, Wisconsin. Now, that's a holy place for you, for there the streets and square, the very air, seem to promote sweetness and light.

The more religious a people are, the less they fuss over death. The Chinese, not greatly religious, make a melodrama of their funerals: assaulting the eyes and ears are the wailing sounds of music, the burning of paper money, the tearing of hair and other acts of ostentatious piety. The Tibetans, deeply religious, throw the corpse into a ravine as food for vultures. Christ dismissed last rites with the shocking, "Let the dead bury the dead." America, no longer a Christian nation, spends inordinately on funerals. Popes, thank God, are still buried in simple pine boxes of the kind used by paupers.

British Airways flight 510 left New York for London on October 9, 1976. There were 164 passengers in economy class, 10 in first class, and a VIP—Nureyev. Five of the meals were vegetarian and two were kosher. In the darkened cockpit, without visual reference points, there was no sense of motion. The aircraft seemed frozen in time and space. A capsule of human domesticity hung thirty thousand feet in the air. Suddenly, First Officer Jevons pointed ahead to his right. "Look." A thin "silver horn rose in the southeastern sky. Captain Cross stared at the apparition and said without affectation: 'That's one of the glories of flying.'"

Meanwhile, the *New York Times* (October 10, 1976) reported, a minor crisis brewed in the passengers' cabin. "An oven had been set aside to heat the kosher meals, but a Jewish passenger was afraid that it had been used on a previous flight to warm non-kosher food." What to do? Certain emergencies were antici-pated: for example, Captain Cross and First Officer Jevons ate "different meals at different times to preclude the possibility of both becoming incapacitated by tainted food." But no one thought of providing an oven so pure that even the most acute religious conscience would be appeased. In the end, the passen-ger ate his meal cold. I wonder who the Creator of Heaven and Earth, the Moth and the Behemoth, would consider the more pious—Captain Cross or the man who ate his meal cold?

Job has much in common with Isaiah, Jeremiah, Micah, and Amos in complaining about man's injustice to man. Job, however, is unique in accusing God himself of injustice. Why does he un-dergo such grotesque suffering—from death of his children to boils on his body—when he has followed all God's command-ments? God's answer is curiously unimaginative: he cures Job of his boils and restores his children by twice the original number, as though to say, "Oops, sorry about the boils and, ah yes, the children, here are some freshly made ones that are even prettier than the ones I have taken away from you." Can one set of chil-dren be replaced by another—just like cattle? In the end, God recognizes that restitution isn't really the answer. What is the answer then? What can he say or do that will silence Job once and for all? Well, as we know, his final and overwhelming reply is to point to the majesty, the splendor, the mind-boggling diver-sity of creation—of which Job, with his passion for justice, is part, alongside the lion, the raven, the ostrich, the hawk, the rain and the dew, the sea and the stars.

Is God saying that his creation is ultimately aesthetic, that justice itself is *fairness*, a concept of balance and harmony that is a type of the aesthetic? The aesthetic is, however, more than balance and harmony, justice and beauty. It is also the sublime, which contains the idea that order and balance may be breached in the interest of emergence and creativity. The sublime is excess. Job understands justice and beauty, but has difficulty with excess. Isn't generosity itself a type of excess, a gesture, an action—whether initiated by God or by man—that goes beyond justice?

Metaphysical horror—the sense of the vast emptiness of the universe—is one path to religious feeling, even though, initially, it can only be one of despair. But how many people know metaphysical horror? Very few, I should think. Pascal's dread before the eternal silence of infinite space is the classic example. Among moderns, the novelist John Updike is clearly haunted by metaphysical horror: in stories and novels, the hero, whether he is relieving himself in an outhouse or being entertained in a movie theater, is suddenly confronted by the icy cold and stellar dust of a universe that is utterly indifferent to his wrestling with constipation, or with the chewing gum that stubbornly refuses to be dislodged from the sole of his shoe.

But then again, metaphysical horror may not be all that rare. Any intelligent child who has read an astronomy book or two can have it. I am so reminded by a 1995 movie called *The Cure.* It is a charming story of two eleven-year-olds—Erik, a big-sized mesomorph and a bit of a bully, and Dexter, a frail intellectual dying of AIDS—sailing down the Mississippi in search of a cure. Camping in a small tent along the bank of the river, Erik was wakened in the middle of the night by sounds of moaning. He woke his companion to find him shivering and drenched in sweat. Erik removed Dexter's wet shirt and put his dry one on him. Dexter, somewhat comforted but still frightened by premonition of death, explained that he had a nightmare in which he was alone billions of miles from Earth, and that there was absolutely nothing out there and that he couldn't possibly hope to get back. Erik's response was to pick up one of his gym shoes, put it in Dexter's lap, and say something like: "Hold on to it. Go back to sleep. Don't be afraid. Should you find yourself in outer space again, ask: 'Hey, what am I doing with Erik's dirty smelly shoe, and you will be back with me on Earth.'"

And so, what is the answer to metaphysical horror? Religion? Or is it friendship—your friend's shirt on your back, his gym shoe in your lap, when you need them for warmth and consolation?

Horror is not necessarily tied to numbers. One can be numbed by numbers—the 10,000 wiped out in a flood, the 50,000 tortured and killed in crazed genocide, the 25 to 30 million killed in the Chinese civil war of 1851 to 1864. A single event, on the other hand, can shake one's faith in God. Dostoevsky's example (a serf boy hunted down and killed by a nobleman's dog on the nobleman's orders, right in front of the boy's mother) is well known. Nauseatingly evil as that incident is, one might still say, "It is the human being that is evil. God is sullied, of course, for he is the creator. But maybe he can just wiggle out of total responsibility." What I have in mind is a far more common event and has little, if anything, to do with human evil. Its peculiar horror lies, it seems to me, in creation itself—in the grisly accidents of existence. This is the scenario. Children play hide-and-seek in an open field. They rush about, shrieking and laughing. One child finds an abandoned icebox and hides in it, thinking how safe he will be. The wind blows the door shut. At the sound of a click, pitch darkness envelopes the child, and in a matter of minutes—minutes of panic and uncomprehending horror—he suffocates. What kind of prayer can the child offer—and to whom?

A search for God is, or ought to be, a search for the Real. For whatever God is, it cannot be an illusion; it cannot be human wishful thinking. But what is Real? A theoretical physicist may say that it is, ultimately, a set of equations and not at all what people normally consider real, which is something tangible and resistant. To the Sufi adept, the Real is even less tangible than mathematical equations—or "poorer," to use a social-religious term. And so if God comes dressed in them, one must continue to look beyond, as the following parable suggests.

In one of the great court banquets, everyone was seated according to rank, waiting for the entry of the king. In came a plain, shabby man who took a seat above everyone else. His boldness angered the prime minister, who ordered the newcomer to identify himself. Was he a minister? No. More. Was he the king? No. More. "Are you then God?" asked the prime minister. "I am above that also," said the shabby man. "There is nothing above God," retorted the prime minister. "That nothing," came the reply, "is me."

But there is another view. The real is solid, compared with which the world of daily experience is like a dream, living in a dense fog, or suffering from a bad head cold. Let me drive the metaphor home with a story. In the Second World War, British warships sailed at night and sometimes in a thick fog along the coast of Norway, which had fallen under Nazi sway. The ship's only guide was the radar screen, yet with it, the ship did remarkably well. It did not go astray or run into a rock. One can imagine the sailors coming around to the view that those flashes of light on the screen were all that constituted reality. What else was there? Indeed, what need was there for more? Early next morning, the fog lifted. The sailors went on deck. They breathed in the fresh air and were amazed to see around them a sea specked with white foam, beautiful islands, a jagged coast draped in waterfalls, and the sun ascending the blue sky. Now that's reality! To think that they had almost forgotten it in the dim hold of the ship. The theological point is that we are like the sailors: we are so habituated to our fuzzy and limited vision that we mistake it for reality. One day—perhaps only after death—we shall see it as it truly is, solid and brilliant.

"When you have learned that you are immortal, will that be enough for you?" Augustine asked himself in *Soliloquia*. His immodest answer: "It will be something great, but it is too little for me."

Great thinkers who propelled the West into the modern age (among them Descartes, Spinoza, Robespierre, Kant, Fichte, Goethe) believed in the immortality of the soul and in the Supreme Being. How come? we ask. Weren't they the guys who sought to destroy religion and its superstitions? Yes, they were against institutional religion and almost all its doctrines, but they retained a belief that had its roots in classical antiquity and, indeed, beyond it in the great Eastern religions, outstandingly, Hinduism. Without this belief, captured by the phrase "immortality of the soul," it is hard to imagine how Western man could have had the confidence and the courage to venture into such strange seas of thought as Newtonian mechanics, Einsteinian physics, human equality, and universal rights.

"Immortality of the soul" derives from a belief in something called soul (atman, spirit, reason) that is imprisoned in the material body, from which it seeks to escape to be reunited with Brahman, God, or the Supreme Being. The body, necessarily limited by its sensory equipment and racked moreover by passion, is the source of illusion and error. How to be freed from it and rise to the realm of reality and truth? Hindus asked this question, as did Plato and Platonists, Stoics—Greek and Roman—and, surprisingly, revolutionary modern thinkers. Thus Marcus Aurelius (121–80), Roman emperor and Stoic: "You are a little soul bearing about a corpse." Doesn't this have a Hindu flavor, and isn't it much the same as Descartes's belief that man is an "angelic" being of pure spirit, which by chance and irrelevantly dwells in the body? And then there is Kant, for whom the immortality of the soul is the continuing of the rational being into infinity, once it is shorn of its limitations and the indigence of physical life. (See Josef Pieper, *Death and Immortality*.)

But isn't it absurd—contrary to all human experience—that the rational being (something like mind or spirit) can continue apart from the body? How could a great thinker like Kant, and before him Descartes, entertain any such notion? Well, they could because somehow, in the late seventeenth century, atman, soul, and spirit had mutated into reason, which was regarded as a transcendental power capable of apprehending the first principles of truth *apart from* empirical evidence. By the eighteenth century, reason would seem to have assumed the role and prestige of such older terms as *soul* and *spirit*. Even though thinkers continued to say "immortality of the soul," they really meant "immortality of reason." Reason was immortal—it did not suffer decay as the body did—because it had the capacity for truth. The capacity for truth was divine. Reason had to be divine—had to lie outside the realm of nature—for it to judge whether any picture of it, including the picture that reason was a mere product of biological evolution, was true.

The elevation of reason to divinity resulted in rapid progress in all areas of knowledge, particularly mathematics and the physical sciences. But detractors lurked in the wings. Their objections went—and still go—something like this. Reason, if it is divine, is undemocratic, for only a small number of people can have ready access to it. Reason casts a shadow over the life of the senses, where the deepest pleasures lie. It weakens passion that can lead to great achievements, such as wars of conquest and political revolution. In any case, sometime in the nineteenth century, reason was no longer considered an attribute of human beings that made them immortal. But without it, truth itself became problematic, so much so that some thinkers sought to cut the Gordian knot by jettisoning the very idea of truth. All that we need to live well (they say) is practical knowledge, which includes knowing how to get along with one another, not truth—and certainly not capitalized Truth, with its transcendental halo.

In the nineteenth century, Karl Marx led the attack on spirit. He famously reversed Hegel's position, which was traditional to the extent that it elevated spirit. To Marx, spirit and its works (ideas and values) were the largely delusory and ineffective secretions of material forces. However, he retained the Enlightenment's respect for reason and, along with it, respect for truth. We now see this as illogical, because how can truth—*any* possible formulation of it—be respected when it is in the end no more than a material by-product?

A more radical position, called postmodernism, emerged in the dying decades of the twentieth century. After millennia of elevating spirit above body, culminating in the cult of divine reason during the Enlightenment, spirit is at last firmly put back in its place—reabsorbed into body, which is given an epistemological status it never had before. Body is not only an Eden, full of sensorial delights, but also the instrument of knowledge. All that we can know is known through its capabilities and limitations. Postmodern feminists make much of the fact that the body is gendered: man and woman see the world differently. Once this difference is highlighted, however, there is nothing to prevent one from going on to recognize that, in the end, every body is unique, that every embodied being has a different take on reality. How, then, is bonding and communication among human individuals possible? Postmodernism, which begins reasonably enough with an attack on the abstractness of the generalized noun *body*, seems to end in solipsism—in a world of barely communicating individuals, each trapped in his or her body.

Understandably, postmodernist thinkers choose not to follow this path. Instead, they turn their attention to the collective body, for example, an ethnic or cultural group. Differences among individuals are thankfully forgotten in the identity of the collective body—the group. As for differences among groups, they make intergroup communication difficult, but this, far from generating a sense of isolation, has the effect of generating a strong sense of identity and pride within each group. Another consequence of postmodernist thought is this: by denigrating spirit and its highest achievements, the cultural works that remain (clothes, food ways, folk dances, songs, vernacular architecture, and so on)—all tethered more or less to the needs of the individual or social body or both—can be on show without inviting the judgment that one work is superior to another. In other words, the postmodernist posture both reflects and encourages Western society's strong desire for egalitarianism.

The elevation of the body, collective and individual, at the expense of spirit is problematic. How is one to glorify the collective body when whatever outstanding achievements it has are tagged as hegemonic and in need of deconstruction? As for the individual human body, glorifying it runs against the indisputable fact that it is subject to decay and eventually dies. The best one can do is to prolong its life for as long as possible, with all the scientific marvels at one's command. Ironically, these scientific marvels are themselves the products of a time when reason was divine—a proud descendant and transmutation of atman, spirit, and the "immortal soul."

How do we see other human beings? How should we treat them? Many books on theology and moral philosophy—and, for that matter, many books on etiquette—tell us how. But in boldness and eloquence, none to my knowledge comes close to the reply that C. S. Lewis gave in a university sermon ("The Weight of Glory," *Theology*, November 1941):

> It is a serious thing to live in a society of possible gods and goddesses, to remember that the dullest and most uninteresting person you talk to may one day be a creature which, if you saw it now, you would be strongly tempted to worship, or else a horror and a corruption such as you now meet, if at all, only in a nightmare. All day long we are, in some degree, helping each other to one or other of these destinations. It is in the light of these overwhelming possibilities, it is with awe and the circumstances proper to them, that we should conduct all our dealings with one another, all friendships, all loves, all play, all politics. There are no ordinary people. You have never talked to a mere mortal. Nations, cultures, arts, civilizations—these are mortal, and their life is to ours as the life of a gnat. But it is immortals whom we joke with, marry, snub, and exploit— immortal horrors or everlasting splendors. This does not mean that we are to be perpetually solemn. We must play.

But our merriment must be of that kind (and it is, in fact, the merriest kind) which exists between people who have, from the outset, taken each other seriously—no flippancy, no superiority, no presumption.

How far we have fallen from this exalted, religious conception of the human person! Men and women nowadays seek self-esteem and dignity in their own culture. Culture? Even great civilizations, to an older way of thinking, are transients (gnats) compared to who we are. C. S. Lewis was hardly alone. When I was an undergraduate in the late 1940s, his view of the human being was shared by some of the finest intellects of the time. Odd is the fact that they were all Christians: J. R. R. Tokien and T. S. Eliot in England, Reinhold Niebuhr and (later) Paul Tillich in the United States, Emil Brunner in Germany, Gabriel Marcel and Jacques Maritain in France, Albert Schweitzer in Lambaréné. I say odd, for, a few decades later, the word *Christian* connotes intellectual backwardness.

Impending death or affliction can be a purifying experience. No one has ever said that good fortune is purifying or ennobling. So, perhaps it is of small account?

Religious experience, for me, is the intoxicating moment when I feel that good matters overwhelmingly and evil is contemptible, and when I can say with the utmost conviction, "Now, at last, I understand." It is also the moment when I feel totally safe.

Stages of Life

A frustrated human infant turns lobster-pink and can scream for ten minutes or more. Do the infants of other species show comparable rage when they don't get what they want? I believe not. The screaming infant is repellent to everyone other than its besotted parents. And yet, isn't this rage the first sign of a divine (satanic?) discontent, an arrogant refusal to adapt that drives the human being to create a world that, at a turn of the prayer wheel or a flip of the electric switch, responds to his every need?

A young child stares. A well-mannered older child doesn't. Instead, he looks at you with a twinkle in his eyes. Charming, yes, but that twinkle already signifies a loss of innocence. Do a dog's eyes twinkle?

For a person to be happy, time must seem oceanic, endless. Young children often feel that way. Adults? Well, on a hot summer afternoon, when a small airplane drones in the distance—a tiny dot that hangs almost motionless in the clear blue sky—time can seem unbounded too.

First experiences are fresh and exciting. They are the special privilege of a child. What about last experiences? Don't they also have a certain keenness? Last experiences—for example, the trip to Nepal that is unlikely to be repeated because of one's age—are a privilege of the old. It is people in the middle span who are in trouble. Experience, for them, has neither the freshness of "first time," nor the wistful keenness of "last time." Repetition—even the prospect of repetition—can take the edge off experience.

In C. S. Lewis's novel *Out of the Silent Planet*, the earthling Ransom wants to know why a *hross*, an intelligent denizen of the planet Malacandra (Mars), has no compulsion to repeat a delightful experience. On Earth people want to have their pleasure again and again like greedy children; they are not content with mere remembrance. The *hross* is puzzled, for to him a pleasure is full grown only when it is remembered: "What you can remember is the last part of the pleasure, as the *crab* is the last part of a poem. When you and I met, the meeting was over very shortly, it was nothing. Now it is growing into something as we remember it. But still we know very little about it. What it will be when I remember it as I lie down to die . . . that is the real meeting. The other is only [its] beginning."

We tend to agree with Proust that memory is "retracing by moonlight the roads on which we once played in the sun." Yet, as Lewis argues, memory can be far more substantial than waning moonlight. If vivid, transient pleasure is a privilege of the child, then rich, enduring pleasure—drawing on memory and enlivened by imagination—is a privilege of the adult.

Montaigne (1533–92) sometimes asked his maid to wake him partially at an early morning hour just so that he could slip back deliciously into oblivion. For different reasons, neither the very young nor the very old can enjoy this pleasure. The very young plunge into sleep too soon; the very old, once wakened, would not be able to sleep again.

I am constantly amazed by human precocity. Even young children can be accomplished mathematicians, musicians, and poets. But I thought that two things are beyond them: reflection on the fleetingness of time and a mature attitude toward death. Both presuppose experience, and experience is what they lack. I am no longer so sure. A thoughtful thirteen-year-old says (in *The Me Nobody Knows*, edited by Stephen M. Joseph):

> Often I'll be in my room doing homework, when my mind will just wander and I think to myself, "I'm growing old so fast and there's no time in life to really do anything." When I think back five years, when I was eight years old and I can remember specific incidents and specific things that people have said to me I somehow can't believe that it was five years ago when it seems like yesterday.

As for death, Myra Blueblond-Langner's book on dying
leukemic children (*The Private Worlds of Dying Children*) persuades
me that children only four to six years old can already confront
death with realism, courage, considerateness, and humor. A little
girl refuses to take her medicine, prompting the nurse to ask,
"But don't you want to be a doctor when you grow up?" "No" is
the reply. "Then what do you want to be?" Answer: "A ghost."
Jeffrey gives his mother a rough time. Myra (anthropological ob-
server at the hospital), says, "Jeffrey, why do you always yell at
your mother?" His answer: "Then she won't miss me when I'm
gone." A six-year-old boy wakes up from a long nap and sees two
interns by his bed. The boy says with a strained smile, "I fooled
you, I didn't die."

The wise, to cheer us up, like to say that "it is the journey,
not the arrival, that matters." This philosophy fits well with the
Caribbean cruise. People who go on such cruises have no real
destination, just ports of call at which they stop to amuse themselves before going back to where they started. Not very inspir-
ing, is it? But perhaps that's only my Christian prejudice. In
Christian teaching, the arrival—where one arrives—is everything. The journey matters only to the degree that it prepares
one for the arrival.

Flaubert came to dislike *Madame Bovary* for overshadowing his
later works. He also pondered the irony of a creature outliving
its creator. Here he was, aging, his hands already discolored by
liver spots. But that vain and deluded creature Emma Bovary
promises to live forever. In 1882, while Oscar Wilde was having
his portrait painted, he said to the artist, "What a tragic thing it
is. This portrait will never grow older, and I shall. If it was only
the other way." Wilde was not only thinking of himself growing
old; he was also thinking of the mortality of the artist who
painted him: the artist will die, but not his painting. Among
artists, the writer cuts a more tragic figure than the painter, for

a painting, being a material object, does decay: think of *The Last Supper*. A literary work, by contrast, can truly be forever young. You can buy a copy of *The Iliad* right now with the smell of ink still on it.

Young children struggle to keep awake. Their commitment to waking life is awesome. Older children already begin to feel it a burden. When the teens roll around, the weight of time is such that they seek relief in drugs, alcohol, and sex. The unbearable emptiness at the core must somehow be plugged with the wool of oblivion or the throb of sensation. And so too with grown-ups who fear death and will do almost anything to live a few years longer, yet don't know what to do with the time they already have other than to kill it.

What if one were Mozart? Was there—is there—anyone more talented and healthy-minded? Yet even Mozart was oppressed by the void at the core of his being. Coming back from a concert tour in Berlin, Mozart wrote to his wife, Constanze, in September 1790: "If people could see into my heart, I should almost feel ashamed. To me everything is cold as ice. Perhaps if you were with me I might possibly take more pleasure in the kindness of those I meet here [Frankfurt]. But as it is, everything seems so empty." How could the darling of Europe and of the Gods feel empty? If even he did, what about us?

Saul Bellow is just a Nobel laureate, not a Mozart, and so can perhaps be excused for his lack of cheer. One day, Bellow was confronted by a Fuller brush man determined to make a sale. Bellow kept shaking his head, eager to get back to his work. Exasperated, the Fuller brush man finally said, "Okay, you can at least accept something as a gift, can't you?" Bellow's dour reply: "I have the gift of life, and it's more than I know what to do with."

Edna St. Vincent Millay says to her friends and foes that of course you can't burn a candle at both ends and expect it to last the night—but what a lovely light it gives! This is how a romantic thinks. But we are not all romantics. Ruth Ellsworth of Minneapolis is more down-to-earth. She tells a reporter that she is "seventy and proud of having lived to be that age." Her satisfaction derives in part from having just enjoyed a Thanksgiving dinner, courtesy of the Little Brothers of the Poor. I can sympathize but do not fully understand. How can one take pride in longevity—in one's robust genes and luck? Moreover, I suspect an ignoble cause at the base of longevity—a temperament that is ungenerous, unwilling to let the candle burn, much less at both ends.

There has to be a point beyond which one is not willing to go, even to survive. For Gandhi, that point was well short of chicken soup. Perhaps a gradation should be established, geared to one's stage in life. A child should feel free to eat just about anything. An adult, as Gandhi said, should stop short of chicken soup. As for someone who has already lived his threescore and ten, bean sprouts and pistachio nuts are the upper limit.

If only . . . if only I had said yes, turned to the right rather than to the left, if only someone smiled rather than frowned at the critical moment. If only. These two words, if nothing else, should remind us of life's vulnerability at any age.

I lost my backpack (with wallet in it) in the Memorial Union. I put it on the seat opposite to mine as I drank my coffee, and then forgot about it when I left. Four hours later, I discovered the loss and rushed back to the union, hoping against hope that I would find the backpack still there, waiting sweetly for me. But of course it wasn't. Nobody took it to the Lost and Found. It had disappeared, along with a book, my lectures notes, and wallet. I missed my wallet most. The book could be replaced. Lecture notes mattered more because they were necessary to me as a teacher. But the wallet was necessary to me as a respectable, functioning adult. I kept thinking, why couldn't the scenario be just a little different? It was so easy for me to imagine myself getting up to leave and a student at another table stopping me to say, "Sir, you have forgotten your backpack." That picture and the subsequent one of me thanking him profusely are so vivid that I can't quite believe that they are just the chimera of wishful thinking.

If reminds us of contingency—the role of tiny forces, many of which are the mere product of chance, in life. What if, in 1959, the young woman to whom I proposed marriage had said yes rather than no—and no because she didn't feel she could make me happy? What if geography student Joshua Hane had stepped on the boulder to the left rather than on the one to the right, which came loose and started an avalanche that killed him?

And, of course, there are the famous ifs of history. If Cleopatra's nose were just a mite longer, the history of the West would have taken a different course, according to Pascal. What if Hitler had not survived childhood smallpox, or if, at an art show, a famous critic had praised his juvenile work? What if Beethoven's mother had miscarried Ludwig and so bestowed on the world only Karl?

An individual's life can be short and dramatic, like a *hogback*, with a steep rise (youth) followed by rapid decline. Or it can be like a *scarpland*, with two possibilities: a long span of steady growth to maturity followed by sharp decline, or a brilliant meteoric rise to success followed by long decline. Finally, an individual's life can be like a *plateau*, whose most distinctive feature is the broad and level top, representing prolonged mature productivity in the course of which encomiums and honors flowed one's way, followed by heart attack, quick onset of senility, and an easy death. That would be my preference.

Modern secularism is full of false good cheer. I am depressed by the relentlessly upbeat literature on old age and find relief in the dour, more realistic view of Montaigne, who noted: "I find old age an increase of envy, injustice, and malice. It stamps more wrinkles on our minds than on our faces; and seldom, or very rarely, does one find souls that do not acquire, as they age, a sour and musty smell. Man moves onward as a whole toward his growth and toward his decay."

In old age, don't become a character. Try to remain a personality. What we call a character—a sweet old man or a doddering old fool—is the result of a thinning of a formerly rich, multifaceted personality. When a carpet wears thin the underside shows through. My own underside is showing—a hard knobby weave in sad contrast to the soft plush that people once knew and appreciated.

To remain healthy, old people have to be active. The easiest way to be active is to make insistent demands—to be, in other words, unpleasant old codgers. Grimley Evans is a gentle and courteous man who teaches gerontology at Oxford. His implausible ambition, reported in *Oxford Today* in 1994, is "to be a thoroughly unpleasant old gentleman, for I'm sure that's the way to a healthier life."

In all the stages of life, I have never lacked heroes and role models. As a boy, I admired athletes and precocious mathematicians; as a young man, I admired great scholars and scientists; in middle age, I sought to keep up with my peers. Now that I am seventy, I need inspiration from octogenarians whose physical decline is compensated by an upward turn in stoic patience and selflessness. But where are they? They are in very short supply, for whereas Mother Nature is prepared to inspire the young and even the mature with appropriate models, she cannot be bothered to do the same for the old, who should in all decency be dead.

Leonardo da Vinci was so keen to pursue his artistic and scientific research that he felt he had to find a way to extend his waking hours. He succeeded by napping fifteen minutes every four hours, limiting his sleep to an hour and a half a day. A researcher recently tested Leonardo's schedule and found that it worked: many of his subjects could reduce their daily sleeping time to under three hours with no adverse effect. An Italian artist followed Leonardo's napping pattern to enhance his own productivity. He got his extra waking hours, but he nevertheless stopped the practice after six months. Why? His answer was that he "didn't know what to do with all his extra free time, since he wasn't another Leonardo." (*Science*, July 20, 1990)

"Old age is the most unexpected thing of all that happens to man," noted Tolstoy a few years before his death. How true. Suddenly I am seventy. Not having married or begotten children—these conspicuous time markers—I thought it not altogether surprising that my life should have slipped by "like wet spinach down the chute" (Harold Nicolson). But, despite the markers, old age caught Tolstoy by surprise.

The image many of us have of ourselves seems to freeze at about age thirty. Time progresses up to that point, then stops, and we remain the same age thereafter. For me, the illusion is particularly striking in the way I keep postponing the reading of certain multivolume classics. "Not now," I say. "Sometime in the future." And I still say it, only to realize with shock that there is only a pencil stump of a future left! I am resigned to not having certain human experiences, from sweaty embrace to seeing the Taj Mahal under moonlight. But I had not thought that some of the greatest ideas of humankind, sitting right there on my bookshelf, would also have to be given up.

I thought old age would bring boredom. Well, it hasn't—at least not yet. It never occurred to me that I have never been old before, that being old can be a novelty. By the time I am tired of being seventy, why, I'll turn seventy-one—and I have never been seventy-one before! It's as simple as that. Add to it the fact that since my retirement at age sixty-eight, I have been getting rid of possessions. Leading a life of steady subtraction rather than of steady accumulation is a novelty too, and I am enjoying the new experience. Of course, as subtraction continues I may get used to it. Moreover, it can become painful, for not only material possessions but also mental ones, which I wish to keep, disappear.

In the course of a long career, I have had to write and rewrite my curriculum vitae many times. It seems to me an increasingly meaningless exercise, for its traditional format does not allow events that have influenced me most—events that have made me into the sort of person I am. In the official vita, I am encouraged to list my place and year of birth, the schools I attended, the institutions at which I taught, my accomplishments, and even my travels, as though these were the true defining moments. But were they? They now seem to me quite arbitrary. Why, for example, include the schools and universities I attended but not the books I read? Did one year at Bloomington, Indiana, two years at Toronto, really matter more to me than the tens and scores of years I have spent, on and off, with certain books?

Now that I've retired, no one badgers me for a copy of my vita. This is the downside. But the upside is that I can at last write it the way I wish. In my ideal vita, I would skip certain geographical residences (mere tourist places for me) in favor of certain writings that have been and are still my home. At age seven, in a one-room school in wartime China, I read Oscar Wilde's fable "The Happy Prince" in Chinese. I thought there was nothing more noble than a prince who, as a consequence of his supreme acts of charity, came to a bad end. I loved the realism—the fact that no good deed goes unpunished. As a teenager, I was a devotee of Dostoevsky and found, in particular, *The Brothers Karamazov* a haven to which I could withdraw in moments of metaphysical and religious doubt. As an undergraduate at Oxford, I found inspiration in the works of C. S. Lewis and Simone Weil, two radically different personalities united in their common yearning for Beauty and the Good. As a graduate student at the University of California at Berkeley, I was enamored with the radicalism of Kierkegaard and the realism of Balzac. In graduate school, I consumed Ernst Cassirer, Susanne Langer, and Maurice Merleau-Ponty. I was at a stage in life when I hungered for a social-geographical science that included emotions, feelings, and thought in its province, and not just material and socio-statistical facts. My other favorite writers were and are Hannah Arendt (especially *The Human Condition*), Iris Murdoch (especially *The Sovereignty of Good*), and Thomas Mann (especially *The Magic Mountain* and a late work, *The Black Swan*). In old age, predictably, I seek to stoke the dying fire in my belly by dipping into novels that contain generous dollops of soft porn. The works of Jean Genet, John Updike, Alan Hollinghurst, and Pier Paolo Pasolini satisfy me in that regard.

Before I began to give away my books in preparation for retirement, I always felt a tinkling of excitement—a sort of nervousness and pleasure—when someone looked over my personal library. The book titles alone (their range and number) reveal the human being I am with an explicitness and fullness that no other medium can remotely match. After all, one is what one eats, and I've eaten omnivorously (no literary vegetarian, I) these books.

A Sense of Ending

Afraid of dying? Yes, but I can't disentangle that fear from the fear of embarrassment. I won't know how to behave. My body takes over and does things that make me feel ashamed. No one in my circle ever talks about dying, much less try to describe how he or she may feel when the time comes. So I was much comforted, as one would be in the presence of an intimate friend, when I chanced upon the following passage written by Thomas Browne in 1635: "I am not so much afraid of death, as ashamed thereof. It is the very disgrace and ignominy of our natures, that

213

in a moment can so disfigure us that our nearest friends, wife and children stand and start at us." (*Religio Medici,* part 1, section 38)

Here are three expressions of regret as death looms, two from real human beings, one from literature. A nineteen-year-old RAF pilot, as his Spitfire plunged toward the sea during the Battle of Britain, thought with anguished regret that he was still a virgin. C. S. Lewis made sure that he had read Plato's *Symposium* in the original Greek, for he thought it ridiculous to die without having done so. On her deathbed, the heroine of Honoré de Balzac's novel *Le Lys dans la vallée* regretted deeply that she had led an exemplary life.

The following four deaths have made me sit up, though for very different reasons. Marc Quinquandon, twenty-seven, of Nancy, France, died of indigestion after eating six dozen snails in three minutes and four seconds (*Minneapolis Tribune,* November 27, 1979). A teacher in England who won $1.6 million in a football pool planned to retire in a spending spree but died before he had a chance to do so: "Harry Johnson, 56, was stricken with a heart attack Tuesday while on the way to his woodwork classes, which he had taught for twenty-five years" (*Minneapolis Tribune,* December 7, 1979). Jean-Paul Sartre died, surrounded by close friends (Simone de Beauvoir among them) and relatives. Would he have approved of such a bourgeois ending? Albert Camus, a philosophical novelist who often spoke of the absurd, died more appropriately. He died in a car crash. In his coat pocket was a train ticket. He apparently changed his mind and decided to go by car at the last minute.

On Friday, November 22, 1963, three famous men died: John F. Kennedy, Aldous Huxley, and C. S. Lewis. The young president's violent death so dominated the world's attention that the deaths of the other two barely registered. All three deaths were good deaths. It is heartless to call Kennedy's death a good one, yet from his point of view, what a way to go—at the peak of his fame and power, never to be diminished by the bathos of playing golf in retirement and solitaire in extreme old age. Christopher Isherwood visited Aldous Huxley as he lay dying. Although he was in obvious discomfort, Huxley showed a lively interest in the subjects his visitor brought up—all except death. Isherwood described his friend's ending as "a picture of a great vessel sinking quietly into the deep; many of its delicate marvelous mechanisms still in perfect order, all its lights still shining." What a way for an intellectual to go! Lewis died without fuss, even cozily, as he would have liked it. He had breakfast and answered four letters. He felt sleepy after lunch and was advised by his brother, Warnie, to go to bed. Warnie brought him tea at four and found him still very drowsy but calm and cheerful. An hour and a half later, Warnie heard a crash and ran into the room. He found his brother lying at the foot of the bed, unconscious. He was still breathing, but ceased to do so some three or four minutes later.

As a child I envied other children's popularity. As an adult I envied other people's vitality and requited love. Now that I am old, I envy other people's manner of death. But I am being frivolous. "Men must endure their going hence" (*King Lear*)—the epitaph on Lewis's gravestone.

The death of Socrates is so convincing. Evening comes, Socrates takes the poison, his feet grow cold, followed by his stomach and then his chest, as he slips gently into oblivion. But, alas, his disquisition on immortality isn't convincing. Not even the greatest philosopher can argue me, nor anyone else, into belief. A great novelist, on the other hand, might just do it. I think of Tolstoy's *The Death of Ivan Ilyich*. Tolstoy doesn't argue. Rather, he presents an image of goodness—the peasant boy Gerasim who helps the dying Ilyich to relieve himself over the chamber pot—that makes deathlessness seem just, and therefore plausible:

"Gerasim," said Ivan Ilyich in a feeble voice.

Gerasim started, fearing he had done something wrong, and quickly turned his fresh, good-natured, simple, young face, which was showing the first signs of a beard, to the sick man.

"Yes, sir?"

"This must be very unpleasant for you. You must forgive me. I can't help it."

"Oh no, sir!" said Gerasim as he broke into a smile, his eyes and strong white teeth gleaming. "Why shouldn't I help you? You're a sick man."

J. S. Bach was supremely fertile: he produced more than twenty children and sheaves of immortal music. Yet he was in love with death. He wrote such somber cantatas as "Come sweet death" and "Christ lay in the bonds of death." He also wrote "Heaven laughs, the Earth rejoices"—his Easter Sunday cantata. This music too was somber, for it celebrated death as a gateway to joy and eternal life. In our post-Christian age, we find this welcoming of death incomprehensible—morbid. Or are *we* the morbid ones, with our pathetic hanging on to life no matter how diminished, for it is all that we have?

Eugène Ionesco disdained the old man who hangs on to life, who makes living a little longer his vocation. In *Fragments of a Journal* he depicts a dining-room neighbor thus:

He chews his food slowly, his walnuts and hazelnuts, in the way he's been told is good for him. He's quite revolting. He knows, or he believes that what he eats is giving him life. One mouthful, two hours of life; another mouthful, two more hours of life; by the end of the meal he's sure he has won another week of life. But it's chiefly the look in his eyes that is intolerable, the expression of a healthy old man, sharp, cunning and ferocious. I asked to sit at another

table; that dogged determination to live, the way he clings
to life and won't let go, seems to me tragic, frightening
and immoral.

"Every day is a good day to be born, every day is a good day
to die," said Pope John XXIII on his deathbed. To die, maybe, but
not to be dead. For *to die* delusively suggests activity, a process
that isn't final and that one might almost choose to do. But *to be
dead* is final—though not (perhaps) for the pope.

A 1981 Associated Press photograph shows two brothers
embracing at the Dallas–Fort Worth airport after a separation
of twenty-seven years. It was a Thanksgiving reunion. Also in
the picture, watching the fraternal hug, was twelve-year-old
Steven, the son of one of the brothers. Reason for the reunion?
One brother was dying of cancer. I look at the picture and can
see that the frail elderly man will not live long. The face of his
young nephew, by contrast, seems full of life. Yet only a few
minutes after the photo was taken, the boy collapsed on the
floor and died. Would a fiction writer dare to invent such an unexpected turn?

Schopenhauer: "Herodotus relates that Xerxes wept at the
sight of his army, which stretched further than the eye could
reach, in the thought that of all these, after a hundred years, not
one would be alive. And in looking over a huge catalogue of new
books, one might weep at thinking that, when ten years have
passed, not one of them will be heard of."

Photographs, says Roland Barthes, thrust home the fact of our
mortality. We look at faces and limbs warm or tense with life,
knowing full well that they are now dust. Sound haunts me even
more. I can look at a photo of Maria Callas and accept the fact

that she is dead, but I am bewildered when I hear her voice coming out of my CD player. For that voice, quivering with immediacy and passion, is the quintessence of life—of what it means to be fully alive.

Oliver Reed, the actor who played the important role of Proximo in the film epic *Gladiator,* died of a heart attack on May 2, 1999, before he could complete his part. He was sixty-one years old. His colleagues and friends on the set were shocked and saddened by his unexpected departure. But the play must go on, and, fortunately, technology was there to help. One technique involved taking the earlier shots of Reed and putting them into new backgrounds for the scenes he had left to do, in some cases changing the color of his costume. Another technique involved selecting from previous shots close-ups of Reed's head that could be used on another actor's body. As the director, Ridley Scott, put it: "I had his body double walk up to the camera, stand, and talk, and then I put Oliver's [computer-generated] head on the body." The result was a bravura last turn! Reed, watching from heaven, would have been pleased.

Walter Benjamin suggests that storytelling is stimulated by a circumstance that was, but no longer is, common: witnessing the death of a person one knows. The completion of a life would seem to demand some sort of accounting. When death rubbed shoulders with life everywhere, as during the Middle Ages, it could be that no elaborate accounting was called for. Moreover, many in that period died too young for much of a story to be told. In the Victorian period, people lived longer and death was less intrusive, yet it was still common enough to be almost an annual event in the home. These circumstances favored the development of narrative skills. People learned to tell good stories, hanging richly detailed incidents on the natural curves of completed lives. In our time, the urge or excuse to narrate at length has been eroded by the rarity of attending a relative's or friend's death. It is difficult to make a rounded tale out of someone whom one barely knows, or who is still alive. The best one can do is to pick out and relate isolated incidents—in other words, gossip.

The artist in us insists on appropriate endings. At the end of a party we stand near the door to say good-bye, taking our time over it because we can't find the right word for a gracious exit. What about an entire life? If only we can script a wonderful exit line that will be an inspiration to those who watch us die. More likely, our last bequeathal is the death rattle and the stench of a body already in decay.

"More light!" Grand last words attributed to Goethe. But I prefer those with a bit more humor. "A watched kettle never boils," said a dying person to his solicitous friends gathered around him. And the following story shows Zen Buddhism at its best. A Zen master lay dying, surrounded by disciples who tried to persuade him to swallow a piece of rice cake, which he succeeded in doing after much effort. The end was near. The disciples bent over to catch their master's last words, which were: "My, that tastes good!"

Mircea Eliade, the distinguished historian of religion, had a very large library. When he retired, he disposed of it eagerly in order to have space, as he put it, "on my shelves for *my* books, manuscripts, and correspondence, the theses and studies about me, etc" (*Journal IV 1979—1985*). In the last year of his life, E. B. White lost all interest in books—except those he had written himself. He asked his son to read them to him, one by one (*New Yorker*, December 27, 1993).

Now, I find this pathetic—this shrinking of life to the tiny world that one has made oneself. Yet, why? After all, in retirement and old age, it is perfectly acceptable to cut loose acquaintances and even friends in order to have more time for family. In the ideal deathbed scene, the dying man is surrounded by his children and grandchildren. So what's wrong with a writer dying in the company of his brain children and grandchildren?

Jan Hendrik van den Berg, a Dutch physician, argues in *Medical Power and Medical Ethics* against the senseless prolongation of life in old and dying people. Death should be allowed to arrive in a way suited to the life that was lived. "Death," he writes, "is not the period at the end of a sentence; it is the last word. The meaning of the whole sentence depends on the last word. What gives the doctor the right to take away the patient's last word and to replace it by another word that is not his own?"

Several years ago, National Public Radio gave a detailed account of a Texas prisoner's last day before execution: a session with his attorney; a final appeal to the governor; visits by friends and relatives; the traditional last meal, which, on request, consisted of fried shrimp with a side dish of cole slaw; a visit with the chaplain; and then the trip to the execution chamber, where, with prison officials, chaplain, and physician looking on, he was given a lethal injection.

An unexpected emotion—envy—welled up in me as I listened to the report. How will I, an upright citizen, die? In a car or airplane crash? By gunshot at a service station? Cancer? AIDS? However my life ends, it will be without the support of society: no ceremonial visit by the chaplain, no last meal of my choice, no official on hand to make sure that I die painlessly. For these privileges I must first kill someone. And they say crime doesn't pay!

Suicide is a mistake—a self-deception. The self-deception lies in thinking that one no longer cares about society. One does care. Society's grip is firm to the very end. Consider the two famous bridges of the Bay Area in California, the Golden Gate

Bridge and the Bay Bridge. Both were built around the 1930s; both rise some two hundred feet above the water. A potential suicide can kill himself as easily on the one as on the other. Yet almost a thousand have dived off the Golden Gate Bridge and only a fifth that number off the Bay Bridge. Moreover, whereas several people had driven all the way across the Bay Bridge to jump off the Golden Gate Bridge, none had done so in the opposite direction. Why? Status is surely an important part of the answer. The Bay Bridge is too close to unchic Oakland and lacks, moreover, the Golden Gate's more soaring and glamorous image. What will the neighbors say?

B. F. Skinner says, "At a concert or listening to recorded music I have often found myself impatiently waiting for a piece of music to end, even though I am enjoying it." The reason, he thinks, is that music builds up to a termination that is maximally reenforcing. One waits a little impatiently for the termination that transfigures the entire piece. That's how I see life, not just music. Even as I enjoy life I wait impatiently for it to end—to end, of course, on the right note.

Because I sleep so poorly in old age, I yearn for oblivion. Oblivion in the sense of being totally wiped out, utterly forgotten, has another attraction. It means that I will at last join the majority—my dust mixing with the dust of the billions who have also lived unremarkable and unnoted lives.

"I have always depended on the kindness of strangers." I like the ending of Tennessee Williams's *A Streetcar Named Desire* because, to me, the two moral jewels of civilization are the kindness of strangers and impersonal justice. Another ending I like is in T. S. Eliot's *The Cocktail Party*. Edward and Lavinia wait nervously for their party to begin. They fuss over last-minute details. The sandwich tray is in place. Edward says, "It will soon be over."

Lavinia says, "I wish it would begin." Then the doorbell rings.
Lavinia's last words (and the play's) are: "Oh, I'm glad. It's begun."
One of the good things about life, as about the cocktail party, is
that it does eventually come to an end, and it is the promise of
an end that makes the beginning and the middle not only bear-
able, but enjoyable.

~·

Each life is a musical theme, implanted by God or nature. Our
duty is to enrich and elevate it with as many variations as possible. But there is a limit to the number we can produce, after
which it is best to simply stop, and say to God, "There I have
done my best." Remember, even Beethoven could ring only
thirty-three variations on a theme by Diabelli.

~·

"Determination," said Paul Goodman, "is the will to termi-
nate." Anyone can start a project, but the professional, unlike the
amateur, finishes. Isn't this how art differs from life? Some of us
are professionals in art, but all of us are amateurs in life. In life,
neither the beginning nor the end is within our control; we can
shape, if we are lucky, only the middle. Any exceptions? Yes,
Senator Hubert Horatio Humphrey, for one. His last days
rounded off a life like the last chapter of an uplifting Victorian
novel. At Waverly, his country estate by the lake, the dying
senator was surrounded by wife, children, and grandchildren.
Physicians and nurses were in constant attendance. In the midst
of this idyllic setting, the senator nobly sought to resolve the
Middle East crisis by making a last personal appeal to Prime
Minister Begin of Israel. What a way to go!

Leo Tolstoy's last days were full of self-doubt and anguish.
He didn't die at his country estate; he died in a country railway
station. If I had the courage of my convictions, I would want to
die like Tolstoy. To put it a little differently, although I try to
make this book end with the satisfactory roundness of art, like
Hubert Humphrey's last days, I should not mind—I would feel
more a part of common humanity—if my life ends raggedly,

with loose strings that are meant to go somewhere but will remain forever untied.

Looking at the stars always makes me dream.... Why, I ask myself, shouldn't the shining dots of the sky be as accessible as the black dots on the map of France? Just as we take the train to get to Tarascon or Rouen, we take death to reach a star.

—Vincent Van Gogh

Yi-Fu Tuan was born in Tianjin, China. He attended school in China, Australia, and the Philippines, and earned degrees from Oxford University and the University of California at Berkeley. He has taught at Indiana University, the University of New Mexico, the University of Toronto, the University of Minnesota, and the University of Wisconsin at Madison, where he retired in 1998 from his position as Vilas Professor of Geography. He is author of *Escapism* and *Who Am I? An Autobiography of Emotion, Mind, and Spirit,* as well as ten other books. His interests span the range of the social sciences and the humanities, with a focus on the central geographical themes of space and place.